MARRIAGE À LA MODE:
A COMEDY.

by

John Dryden

—*Quicquid sum ego, quamvis*
Infra Lucili censum ingeniumque, tamen me
Cum magnis vixisse, invita fatebitur usque
Invidia, et fragili quærens illidere dentem,
Offendet solido.

Horat. Serm.

WITH THE RESTORED MUSIC OF

ROBERT SMITH

&

NICHOLAS STAGGINS

from the manuscript *Choice Songs and Ayres for One Voyce*,
originally published 1673

A.D. 2010

MARRIAGE À-LA-MODE

PROLOGUE.

Lord, how reformed and quiet are we grown,
Since all our braves and all our wits are gone!
Fop-corner now is free from civil war,
White-wig and vizard make no longer jar.
France, and the fleet, have swept the town so clear,
That we can act in peace, and you can hear.
'Twas a sad sight, before they marched from home,
To see our warriors in red waistcoats come,
With hair tucked up, into our tireing-room.
But 'twas more sad to hear their last adieu:
The women sobbed, and swore they would be true;
And so they were, as long as e'er they could,
But powerful guinea cannot be withstood,
And they were made of play-house flesh and blood.
Fate did their friends for double use ordain;
In wars abroad they grinning honour gain,
And mistresses, for all that stay, maintain.
Now they are gone, 'tis dead vacation here,
For neither friends nor enemies appear.
Poor pensive punk now peeps ere plays begin,
Sees the bare bench, and dares not venture in;
But manages her last half-crown with care,
And trudges to the Mall, on foot, for air.
Our city friends so far will hardly come,
They can take up with pleasures nearer home;
And see gay shows, and gaudy scenes elsewhere;
For we presume they seldom come to hear.
But they have now ta'en up a glorious trade,
And cutting Morecraft struts in masquerade.
There's all our hope, for we shall shew to-day
A masking ball, to recommend our play;
Nay, to endear them more, and let them see
We scorn to come behind in courtesy,
We'll follow the new mode which they begin,
And treat them with a room, and couch within:
For that's one way, howe'er the play fall short,
To oblige the town, the city, and the court.

DRAMATIS PERSONÆ

POLYDAMAS, *Usurper of Sicily.*
LEONIDAS, *the rightful Prince, unknown.*
ARGALEON, *favourite to* POLYDAMAS.
HERMOGENES, *foster-father to* LEONIDAS.
EUBULUS, *his friend and companion.*
RHODOPHIL, *captain of the guards.*
PALAMEDE, *a courtier.*
STRATO, *servant to Palamede's father.*

A MESSENGER

PALMYRA, *daughter to the Usurper.*
AMALTHEA, *sister to* ARGALEON.
DORALICE, *wife to* RHODOPHIL.
MELANTHA, *an affected lady.*
PHILOTIS, *woman to* MELANTHA.
BELIZA, *woman to* DORALICE.
ARTEMIS, *a court lady.*

LADIES, GENTLEMEN, GUARDS, CITIZENS, ATTENDANTS.

SCENE,—*Sicily.*

ACT I.
SCENE I. — *Walks near the Court.*

[*Enter* **Doralice** *and* **Beliza.**]

Dora. Beliza, bring the lute into this arbour; the walks are empty: I would try the song the princess Amalthea bade me learn.

[*They go in, and sing.*]

I.
Why should a foolish marriage vow,
Which long ago was made,
Oblige us to each other now,
When passion is decay'd?
We loved and lov'd, as long as we could,
'Till our love was lov'd out of us both;
But our marriage is dead,
When the pleasure is fled:
'Twas pleasure first made it an oath.
II.
If I have pleasure for a friend,
And further love in store,
What wrong has he, whose joys did end,
And who could give no more?
'Tis a madness that he should be jealous of me,
Or that I should bar him of another:
For all we can gain,
Is to give ourselves pain,
When neither can hinder the other.

[*Enter* **Palamede**, *in a riding-habit, and hears the Song. Re-enter* **Doralice** *and* **Beliza.**]

Beli. Madam, a stranger.

Dora. I did not think to have had witnesses of my bad singing.

Pala. If I have erred, madam, I hope you'll pardon the curiosity of a stranger; for I may well call myself so, after five years absence from the court: but you have freed me from one error.

Dora. What's that, I beseech you?

Pala. I thought good voices, and ill faces, had been inseparable; and that to be fair, and sing well, had been only the privilege of angels.

Dora. And how many more of these fine things can you say to me?

Pala. Very few, madam; for if I should continue to see you some hours longer, you look so killingly that I should be mute with wonder.

Dora. This will not give you the reputation of a wit with me. You traveling monsieurs live upon the stock you have got abroad, for the first day or two: to repeat with a good memory, and apply with a good grace, is all your wit; and, commonly, your gullets are sewed up, like cormorants. When you have regurged what you have taken in, you are the leanest things in nature.

Pala. Then, madam, I think you had best make that use of me; let me wait on you for two or three days together, and you shall hear all I have learnt of extraordinary in other countries; and one thing which I never saw 'till I came home, that is, a lady of a better voice, better face, and better wit, than any I have seen abroad. And, after this, if I should not declare myself most passionately in love with you, I should have less wit than yet you think I have.

Dora. A very plain, and pithy declaration. I see, sir, you have been traveling in Spain or Italy, or some of the hot countries where men come to the point immediately. But are you sure these are not words of course? For I would not give my poor heart an occasion of complaint against me that I engaged it too rashly, and then could not bring it off.

Pala. Your heart may trust itself with me safely; I shall use it very civilly while it stays, and never turn it away, without fair warning to provide for itself.

Dora. First, then, I do receive your passion with as little consideration, on my part, as ever you gave it me, on yours. And now, see what a miserable wretch you have made yourself!

Pala. Who, I miserable? Thank you for that. Give me love enough, and life enough, and I defy Fortune.

Dora. Know, then, thou man of vain imagination, know, to thy utter confusion, that I am virtuous.

Pala. Such another word, and I give up the ghost.

Dora. Then, to strike you quite dead, know that I am married too.

Pala. Art thou married? O thou damnable virtuous woman!

Dora. Yes, married to a gentleman; young, handsome rich, valiant, and with all the good qualities that will make you despair, and hang yourself.

Pala. Well, in spite of all that, I'll love you: Fortune has cut us out for one another; for I am to be married within these three days; married, past redemption to a young, fair, rich, and virtuous lady; and it shall go hard but I will love my wife as little, as, I perceive, you do your husband.

Dora. Remember, I invade no propriety: my servant you are, only 'till you are married.

Pala. In the meantime, you are to forget you have a husband.

Dora. And you, that you are to have a wife.

Beli. [*aside, to her Lady.*] O madam, my lord's just at the end of the walks; and, if you make not haste, will discover you.

Dora. Some other time, new servant, we'll talk further of the premises; in the meanwhile, break not my first commandment, that is, not to follow me.

Pala. But where, then, shall I find you again?

Dora. At court. Yours, for two days, sir.

Pala. And nights, I beseech you, madam.

[*Exeunt* **Doralice** *and* **Beliza.**]

Pala. Well, I'll say that for thee, thou art a very dexterous executioner; thou hast done my business at one stroke: yet I must marry another — and yet I must love this; and if it lead me into some little inconveniencies, as jealousies, and duels, and death, and so forth — yet, while sweet love is in the case, Fortune, do thy worst, and avaunt, mortality!

[*Enter* **Rhodophil**, *who seems speaking to one within.*]

Rhod. Leave 'em with my lieutenant, while I fetch new orders from the king.
[*Sees* **Palamede.**]
— How? Palamede!

Pala. Rhodophil!

Rhod. Who thought to have seen you in Sicily?

Pala. Who thought to have found the court so far from Syracuse?

Rhod. The king best knows the reason of the progress. But, answer me, I beseech you, what brought you home from travel?

Pala. The commands of an old rich father.

Rhod. And the hopes of burying him?

Pala. Both together, as you see, have prevailed on my good nature. In few words, my old man has already married me; for he has agreed with another old man, as rich and as covetous as himself; the articles are drawn, and I have given my consent, for fear of being disinherited; and yet know not what kind of woman I am to marry.

Rhod. Sure your father intends you some very ugly wife, and has a mind to keep you in ignorance till you have shot the gulf.

Pala. I know not that; but obey I will, and must.

Rhod. Then I cannot choose but grieve for all the good girls and courtesans of France and Italy. They have lost the most kind-hearted, doting, prodigal humble servant, in Europe.

Pala. All I could do, in these three years I stayed behind you, was to comfort the poor creatures for the loss of you. But what's the reason that, in all this time, a friend could never hear from you?

Rhod. Alas, dear Palamede! I have had no joy to write, nor indeed to do any thing in the world to please me. The greatest misfortune imaginable is fallen upon me.

Pala. Pr'ythee, what's the matter?

Rhod. In one word, I am married: wretchedly married; and have been above these two years. Yes, faith, the devil has had power over me, in spite of my vows and resolutions to the contrary.

Pala. I find you have sold yourself for filthy lucre; she's old, or ill conditioned.

Rhod. No; none of these: I'm sure she's young; and, for her humour, she laughs, sings, and dances eternally; and, which is more, we never quarrel about it, for I do the same.

Pala. You're very unfortunate indeed: then the case is plain, she is not handsome.

Rhod. A great beauty too, as people say.

Pala. As people say? Why, you should know that best yourself.

Rhod. Ask those, who have smelt to a strong perfume two years together, what's the scent.

Pala. But here are good qualities enough for one woman.

Rhod. Ay, too many, Palamede. If I could put them into three or four women, I should be content.

Pala. O, now I have found it! You dislike her for no other reason but because she's your wife.

Rhod. And is not that enough? All that I know of her perfections now, is only by memory. I remember indeed, that about two years ago I loved her passionately; but those golden days are gone, Palamede: Yet I loved her a whole half year, double the natural term of any mistress; and I think, in my conscience, I could have held out another quarter, but then the world began to laugh at me, and a certain shame, of being out of fashion, seized me. At last, we arrived at that point, that there was nothing left in us to make us new to one another. Yet still I set a good face upon the matter, and am infinite fond of her before company; but when we are alone, we walk like lions in a room; she one way, and I another. And we lie with our backs to each other, so far distant, as if the fashion of great beds was only invented to keep husband and wife sufficiently asunder.

Pala. The truth is, your disease is very desperate; but, though you cannot be cured you may be patched up a little: you must get you a mistress, Rhodophil. That, indeed, is living upon cordials; but, as fast as one fails, you must supply it with another. You're like a gamester who has lost his estate; yet, in doing that, you have learned the advantages of play, and can arrive to live upon't.

Rhod. Truth is, I have been thinking on't, and have just resolved to take your counsel; and, faith, considering the damned disadvantages of a married man, I have provided well enough, for a poor humble sinner, that is not ambitious of great matters.

Pala. What is she, for a woman?

Rhod. One of the stars of Syracuse, I assure you: Young enough, fair enough; and, but for one quality, just such a woman as I could wish.

Pala. O friend, this is not an age to be critical in beauty. When we had good store of handsome women, and but few chapmen, you might have been more curious in your choice; but now the price is enhanced upon us, and all mankind set up for mistresses, so that poor little creatures, without beauty, birth, or breeding, but only impudence, go off at unreasonable rates: And a man, in these hard times, snaps at them, as he does at broad gold; never examines the weight, but takes light or heavy, as he can get it.

Rhod. But my mistress has one fault, that's almost unpardonable; for, being a town-lady, without any relation to the court, yet she thinks herself undone if she be not seen there three or four times a day with the princess Amalthea. And, for the king, she haunts and watches him so narrowly in a morning, that she prevents even the chemists, who beset his chamber, to turn their mercury into his gold.

Pala. Yet, hitherto, methinks, you are no very unhappy man.

Rhod. With all this, she's the greatest gossip in nature; for, besides the court, she's the most eternal visitor of the town; and yet manages her time so well, that she seems ubiquitary. For my part, I can compare her to nothing but the sun; for, like him, she takes no rest, nor ever sets in one place, but to rise in another.

Pala. I confess, she had need be handsome, with these qualities.

Rhod. No lady can be so curious of a new fashion, as she is of a new French word: she's the very mint of the nation; and as fast as any bullion comes out of France, coins it immediately into our language.

Pala. And her name is —

Rhod. No naming; that's not like a cavalier: Find her, if you can, by my description; and I am not so ill a painter that I need write the name beneath the picture.

Pala. Well, then, how far have you proceeded in your love?

Rhod. 'Tis yet in the bud, and what fruit it may bear I cannot tell; for this insufferable humour of haunting the court is so predominant, that she has hitherto broken all her assignations with me, for fear of missing her visits there.

Pala. That's the hardest part of your adventure. But, for aught I see, fortune has used us both alike: I have a strange kind of mistress too in court, besides her I am to marry.

Rhod. You have made haste to be in love, then; for, if I am not mistaken, you are but this day arrived.

Pala. That's all one: I have seen the lady already, who has charmed me; seen her in these walks, courted her, and received, for the first time, an answer that does not put me into despair.
[*To them* **Argaleon, Amalthea,** *and* **Artemis.**]

I'll tell you more at leisure my adventures. The walks fill apace, I see. Stay, is not that the young lord Argaleon, the king's favourite?

Rhod. Yes, and as proud as ever, as ambitious, and as revengeful.

Pala. How keeps he the king's favour with these qualities?

Rhod. Argaleon's father helped him to the crown: besides, he gilds over all his vices to the king, and, standing in the dark to him, sees all his inclinations, interests, and humours, which he so times and soothes, that, in effect, he reigns.

Pala. His sister Amalthea, who, I guess, stands by him, seems not to be of his temper.

Rhod. O, she's all goodness and generosity.

Arga. Rhodophil, the king expects you earnestly.

Rhod. 'Tis done, my lord, what he commanded: I only waited his return from hunting. Shall I attend your lordship to him?

Arga. No; I go first another way.
        [*Exit hastily.*]

Pala. He seems in haste, and discomposed.

Amal. [*to* **Rhod.** *after a short whisper.*] Your friend? Then he must needs be of much merit.

Rhod. When he has kissed the king's hand, I know he'll beg the honour to kiss yours. Come, Palamede.

      [*Exeunt* **Rhodophil** *and* **Palamede** *bowing to* **Amalthea.**]

Arte. Madam, you tell me most surprising news.

Amal.   The fear of it, you see,
Has discomposed my brother; but to me,
All, that can bring my country good, is welcome.

Arte. It seems incredible, that this old king,

Whom all the world thought childless,
Should come to search the farthest parts of Sicily,
In hope to find an heir.

Amal. To lessen your astonishment, I will
Unfold some private passages of state,
Of which you are yet ignorant: Know, first,
That this Polydamus, who reigns, unjustly
Gained the crown.

Arte. Somewhat of this I have confusedly heard.

Amal.   I'll tell you all in brief:
Theagenes, our last great king,
Had, by his queen, one only son, an infant
Of three years old, called, after him, Theagenes.
The general, this Polydamus, then married;
The public feasts for which were scarcely past,
When a rebellion in the heart of Sicily
Called out the king to arms.

Arte.   Polydamus
Had then a just excuse to stay behind.

Amal. His temper was too warlike to accept it.
He left his bride, and the new joys of marriage,
And followed to the field. In short, they fought,
The rebels were o'ercome; but in the fight
The too bold king received a mortal wound.
When he perceived his end approaching near,
He called the general, to whose care he left
His widow queen, and orphan son; then died.

Arte. Then false Polydamus betrayed his trust?

Amal. He did; and, with my father's help, — for which
Heaven pardon him! — so gained their soldiers' hearts,
That, in a few days, he was saluted king:
And when his crimes had impudence enough
To bear the eye of day,
He marched his army back to Syracuse.
But see how heaven can punish wicked men,
In granting their desires: The news was brought him,
That day he was to enter it, that Eubulus,
Whom his dead master had left governor,

Was fled, and with him bore away the queen,
And royal orphan; but, what more amazed him,
His wife, now big with child, and much detesting
Her husband's practices, had willingly
                Accompanied their flight.

Arte. How I admire her virtue!

Amal.   What became
Of her, and them, since that, was never known;
Only, some few days since, a famous robber
Was taken with some jewels of vast price,
Which, when they were delivered to the king,
He knew had been his wife's; with these, a letter,
Much torn and sullied, but which yet he knew
To be her writing.

Arte.   Sure, from hence he learned
He had a son?

Amal.   It was not left so plain:
The paper only said, she died in child-bed;
But when it should have mentioned son or daughter,
Just there it was torn off.

Arte.   Madam, the king.

        [*To them* **Polydamus, Argaleon, Guard** *and*
   Attendants.]

Arga. The robber, though thrice racked, confessed no more.
But that he took those jewels near this place.

Poly. But yet the circumstances strongly argue,
That those, for whom I search, are not far off.

Arga. I cannot easily believe it.

Arte. [*Aside.*]   No, you would not have it so.

Poly. Those, I employed, have in the neighbouring hamlet,
Amongst the fishers' cabins, made discovery
Of some young persons, whose uncommon beauty,
And graceful carriage, make it seem suspicious

They are not what they seem: I therefore sent
The captain of my guards, this morning early,
With orders to secure and bring them to me.
[*Enter* **Rhodophil** *and* **Palamede**.]
O, here he is. Have you performed my will?

Rhod. Sir, those, whom you commanded me to bring,
Are waiting in the walks.

Poly. Conduct them hither.

Rhod. First, give me leave
To beg your notice of this gentleman.

Poly. He seems to merit it. His name and quality?

Rhod. Palamede, son to lord Cleodemus of Palermo,
And new returned from travel.

[**Palamede** *approaches, and kneels to kiss the King's hand.*]

Poly. You are welcome.
I knew your father well, he was both brave
And honest; we two once were fellow soldiers
In the last civil wars.

Pala. I bring the same unquestion'd honesty
And zeal to serve your majesty; the courage
You were pleased to praise in him,
Your royal prudence, and your people's love,
Will never give me leave to try, like him,
In civil wars; I hope it may in foreign.

Poly. Attend the court, and it shall be my care
To find out some employment, worthy you.
Go, Rhodophil, and bring in those without.
[*Exeunt* **Rhodophil** *and* **Palamede**. **Rhodophil** *returns again immediately, and with him enter* **Hermogenes, Leonidas,** *and* **Palmyra**.]
Behold two miracles!
[*Looking earnestly on* **Leonidas** *and* **Palmyra**.]

Of different sexes, but of equal form:
So matchless both, that my divided soul
Can scarcely ask the gods a son or daughter,
For fear of losing one. If from your hands,
You powers, I shall this day receive a daughter,
Argaleon, she is yours; but, if a son,
Then Amalthea's love shall make him happy.

Arga. Grant, heaven, this admirable nymph may prove
That issue, which he seeks!

Amal. Venus Urania, if thou art a goddess,
Grant that sweet youth may prove the prince of Sicily!

Poly. Tell me, old man, and tell me true, from whence
    [*To* **Hermogenes.**]
Had you that youth and maid?

Herm.   From whence you had
Your sceptre, sir: I had them from the gods.

Poly. The gods then have not such another gift.
Say who their parents were.

Herm. My wife, and I.

Arga. It is not likely, a virgin, of so excellent a beauty,
        Should come from such a stock.

Amal. Much less, that such a youth, so sweet, so graceful,
Should be produced from peasants.

Herm. Why, nature is the same in villages,
And much more fit to form a noble issue,
Where it is least corrupted.

Poly. He talks too like a man that knew the world,
To have been long a peasant. But the rack
Will teach him other language. Hence with him!
        [*As the* **Guards** *are carrying him away, his peruke falls
        off.*]
Sure I have seen that face before. Hermogenes!
'Tis he, 'tis he, who fled away with Eubulus,
And with my dear Eudoxia.

Herm.   Yes, sir, I am Hermogenes;
And if to have been loyal be a crime,
I stand prepared to suffer.

Poly. If thou would'st live, speak quickly,
What is become of my Eudoxia?
Where is the queen and young Theagenes?
Where Eubulus? and which of these is mine?
               [*Pointing to* **Leonidas** *and* **Palmyra**.]

Herm. Eudoxia is dead, so is the queen,
The infant king, her son, and Eubulus.

Poly. Traitor, 'tis false: Produce them, or —

Herm.   Once more
I tell you, they are dead; but leave to threaten,
For you shall know no further.

Poly. Then prove indulgent to my hopes, and be
My friend for ever. Tell me, good Hermogenes,
Whose son is that brave youth?

Herm. Sir, he is yours.

Poly. Fool that I am! Thou see'st that so I wish it,
And so thou flatter'st me.

Herm.   By all that's holy!

Poly. Again. Thou canst not swear too deeply...

Yet hold, I will believe thee: Yet I doubt.

Herm. You need not, sir.

Arga. Believe him not; he sees you credulous,
And would impose his own base issue on you,
               And fix it to your crown.

Amal. Behold his goodly shape and feature, sir;
Methinks he much resembles you.

Arga. I say, if you have any issue here,
It must be that fair creature;
By all my hopes I think so.

Amal. Yes, brother, I believe you by your hopes,
For they are all for her.

Poly.   Call the youth nearer.

Herm. Leonidas, the king would speak with you.

Poly. Come near, and be not dazzled with the splendour,
And greatness of a court.

Leon. I need not this encouragement;
I can fear nothing but the gods.
And, for this glory, after I have seen
The canopy of state spread wide above
In the abyss of heaven, the court of stars,
The blushing morning, and the rising sun,
What greater can I see?

Poly. This speaks thee born a prince; thou art, thyself,
               [*Embracing him.*]
That rising sun, and shalt not see, on earth,
A brighter than thyself. All of you witness,
That for my son I here receive this youth,
This brave, this — but I must not praise him further,
Because he now is mine.

Leon. [*Kneeling.*]   I wo'not, sir, believe
That I am made your sport;
For I find nothing in myself, but what
Is much above a scorn. I dare give credit
To whatsoe'er a king, like you, can tell me.
Either I am, or will deserve to be, your son.

Arga. I yet maintain it is impossible
This young man should be yours; for, if he were,
Why should Hermogenes so long conceal him,
When he might gain so much by his discovery?

Herm. [*To the King*] I stayed a while to make him worthy, sir,
Of you. But in that time I found

Somewhat within him, which so moved my love,
I never could resolve to part with him.

Leon. [*To* **Argaleon**.] You ask too many questions, and are
Too saucy for a subject.

Arga. You rather over-act your part, and are
                      Too soon a prince.

Leon. Too soon you'll find me one.

Poly.   Enough, Argaleon!
I have declared him mine; and you, Leonidas,
Live well with him I love.

Arga. Sir, if he be your son, I may have leave
To think your queen had twins. Look on this virgin;
Hermogenes would enviously deprive you
Of half your treasure.

Herm.   Sir, she is my daughter.
I could, perhaps, thus aided by this lord,
Prefer her to be yours; but truth forbid
I should procure her greatness by a lie!

Poly. Come hither, beauteous maid: Are you not sorry
Your father will not let you pass for mine?

Palm. I am content to be what heaven has made me.

Poly. Could you not wish yourself a princess then?

Palm. Not to be sister to Leonidas.

Poly. Why, my sweet maid?

Palm.   Indeed I cannot tell;
But I could be content to be his handmaid.

Arga. [*Aside*] I wish I had not seen her.

Palm. [*To* **Leonidas**.] I must weep for your good fortune;
Pray, pardon me, indeed I cannot help it.

Leonidas, — alas! I had forgot,
Now I must call you prince, — but must I leave you?

Leon. [*Aside.*] I dare not speak to her; for, if I should,
I must weep too.

Poly. No, you shall live at court, sweet innocence,
And see him there. Hermogenes,
Though you intended not to make me happy,
Yet you shall be rewarded for the event.
Come, my Leonidas, let's thank the gods;
Thou for a father, I for such a son.

[*Exeunt* **all** *but* **Leonidas** *and* **Palmyra**.]

Leon. My dear Palmyra, many eyes observe me,
And I have thoughts so tender, that I cannot
In public speak them to you: Some hours hence,
I shall shake off these crowds of fawning courtiers,
And then —

[*Exit* **Leonidas**.]

Palm. Fly swift, you hours! You measure time for me in vain,
'Till you bring back Leonidas again.
Be shorter now; and, to redeem that wrong,
When he and I are met, be twice as long!

[*Exit.*]

ACT II.
SCENE I.

[*Enter* **Melantha** *and* **Philotis**.]

Phil. Count Rhodophil's a fine gentleman indeed, madam; and, I think, deserves your affection.

Mela. Let me die but he's a fine man; he sings and dances *en François*, and writes the *billets doux* to a *miracle*.

Phil. And those are no small talents, to a lady that understands, and values the French air, as your ladyship does.

Mela. How charming is the French air! And what an *etourdi bête* is one of our untravelled islanders! When he would make his court to me, let me die but he is just Æsop's ass, that would imitate the courtly French in his *addresses*; but, instead of those, comes pawing upon me, and doing all things so *mal adroit*-ly.

Phil. 'Tis great pity Rhodophil's a married man, that you may not have an honourable intrigue with him.

Mela. Intrigue, Philotis! That's an old phrase; I have laid that word by; *amour* sounds better. But thou art heir to all my cast words, as thou art to my old wardrobe. Oh, count Rhodophil! Ah *mon cher*! I could live and die with him.

[*Enter* **Palamede**, *and a* **Servant**.]

Serv. Sir, this is my lady.

Pala. Then this is she that is to be divine, and nymph, and goddess, and with whom I am to be desperately in love.
[*Bows to her, delivering a letter.*]
This letter, madam, which I present you from your father, has given me both the happy opportunity, and the boldness, to kiss the fairest hands in Sicily.

Mela. Came you lately from Palermo, sir?

Pala. But yesterday, madam.

Mela. [*Reading the letter.*] Daughter, receive the bearer of this letter, as a gentleman whom I have chosen to make you happy. (O Venus, a new servant sent me! And let me die but he has the air of a *gallant homme*!) His father is the rich lord Cleodemus, our neighbour: I suppose you'll find nothing disagreeable in his person or his converse; both which he has improved by travel. The treaty is already concluded, and I shall be in town within these three days; so that you have nothing to do but to obey your careful father.
[*To* **Palamede.**]
Sir, my father, for whom I have a blind obedience, has commanded me to receive your passionate *addresses*; but you must also give me leave to avow, that I cannot merit them from so accomplished a cavalier.

Pala. I want many things, madam, to render me accomplished; and the first and greatest of them is your favour.

Mela. Let me die, Philotis, but this is extremely French; but yet Count Rhodophil — a gentleman, sir, that understands the *grand monde* so well, who has haunted the best *conversations*, and who, in short, has *voyaged*, may pretend to the good graces of a lady.

Pala. [*Aside.*] Hey-day! *Grand monde*! *Conversation*! *Voyaged*! and *Good Graces*! I find my mistress is one of those that run mad in new French words.

Mela. I suppose, sir, you have made the *tour* of France; and, having seen all that's fine there, will make a *considerable* reformation in the rudeness of our court: For let me die, but an unfashioned, untravelled, mere Sicilian, is a *bête*; and has nothing in the world of an *honnête homme*.

Pala. I must confess, madam, that —

Mela. And what new *minuets* have you brought over with you? Their *minuets* are to a *miracle*! And our Sicilian jiggs are so dull and sad to them!

Pala. For minuets, madam —

Mela. And what new plays are there in *vogue*? And who danced best in the last *grand ballet*? Come, sweet servant, you shall tell me all.

Pala. [*Aside.*] Tell her all? Why, she asks all, and will hear nothing. — To answer in order, madam, to your demands —

Mela. I am thinking what a happy *couple* we shall be! For you shall keep up your *correspondence* abroad, and every thing that's new writ, in France, and fine, I mean all that's *delicate,* and *bien tourné,* we will have first.

Pala. But, madam, our fortune —

Mela. I understand you, sir; you'll leave that to me: For the *menage* of a family, I know it better than any lady in Sicily.

Pala. Alas, madam, we —

Mela. Then, we will never make visits together, nor see a play, but always apart; you shall be every day at the king's *levee,* and I at the queen's; and we will never meet, but in the drawing-room.

Phil. Madam, the new prince is just passed by the end of the walk.

Mela. The new prince, sayest thou? *Adieu,* dear servant; I have not made my court to him these two long hours. O, it is the sweetest prince! So *obligeant, charmant, ravissant,* that — Well, I'll make haste to kiss his hands, and then make half a score visits more, and be with you again in a twinkling.

[*Exit running, with* **Philotis**.]

Pala. [*solus.*] Now heaven, of thy mercy, bless me from this tongue! It may keep the field against a whole army of lawyers, and that in their own language, French gibberish. It is true, in the day-time, it is tolerable, when a man has field room to run from it; but to be shut up in a bed with her, like two cocks in a pit, humanity cannot support it. I must kiss all night in my own defence, and hold her down, like a boy at cuffs, and give her the rising blow every time she begins to speak.
[*Enter* **Rhodophil**.]
But here comes Rhodophil. It is pretty odd that my mistress should so much resemble his: The same newsmonger, the same passionate lover of a court, the same — But, *basta,* since I must marry her. I'll say nothing, because he shall not laugh at my misfortune.

Rhod. Well, Palamede, how go the affairs of love? You have seen your mistress?

Pala. I have so.

Rhod. And how, and how? Has the old Cupid, your father, chosen well for you? Is he a good woodman?

Pala. She's much handsomer than I could have imagined: In short, I love her, and will marry her.

Rhod. Then you are quite off from your other mistress?

Pala. You are mistaken; I intend to love them both, as a reasonable man ought to do: For, since all women have their faults and imperfections, it is fit that one of them should help out the other.

Rhod. This were a blessed doctrine, indeed, if our wives would hear it; but they are their own enemies: If they would suffer us but now and then to make excursions, the benefit of our variety would be theirs; instead of one continued, lazy, tired love, they would, in their turns, have twenty vigorous, fresh, and active lovers.

Pala. And I would ask any of them, whether a poor narrow brook, half dry the best part of the year, and running ever one way, be to be compared to a lusty stream, that has ebbs and flows?

Rhod. Ay, or is half so profitable for navigation?

[*Enter* **Doralice**, *walking by, and reading.*]

Pala. 'Ods my life, Rhodophil, will you keep my counsel?

Rhod. Yes: Where's the secret?

Pala. There it is:
　　　　　[*Showing* **Doralice.**]
I may tell you, as my friend, *sub sigillo,* &c. this is that very lady, with whom I am in love.

Rhod. [*Aside.*] By all that's virtuous, my wife!

Pala. You look strangely: How do you like her? Is she not very handsome?

Rhod. [*Aside.*] Sure he abuses me. — Why the devil do you ask my judgment?

Pala. You are so dogged now, you think no man's mistress handsome but your own. Come, you shall hear her talk too; she has wit, I assure you.

Rhod. [*Going back.*] This is too much, Palamede.

Pala. [*Pulling him forward.*] Pr'ythee do not hang back so: Of an old tried lover, thou art the most bashful fellow!

Dora. [*Looking up.*] Were you so near, and would not speak, dear husband?

Pala. [*Aside.*] Husband, quoth a! I have cut out a fine piece of work for myself.

Rhod. Pray, spouse, how long have you been acquainted with this gentleman?

Dora. Who? I acquainted with this stranger? To my best knowledge, I never saw him before.

[*Enter* **Melantha** *at the other end.*]

Pala. [*Aside.*] Thanks, fortune, thou hast helped me.

Rhod. Palamede, this must not pass so. I must know your mistress a little better.

Pala. It shall be your own fault else. Come, I'll introduce you.

Rhod. Introduce me! Where?

Pala. [*Pointing to* **Melantha,** *who swiftly passes over the stage.*] There. To my mistress.

Rhod. Who? Melantha! O heavens, I did not see her.

Pala. But I did: I am an eagle where I love; I have seen her this half hour.

Dora. [*Aside.*] I find he has wit, he has got off so readily; but it would anger me, if he should love Melantha.

Rhod. [*Aside.*] Now, I could even wish it were my wife he loved; I find he's to be married to my mistress.

Pala. Shall I run after, and fetch her back again, to present you to her?

Rhod. No, you need not; I have the honour to have some small acquaintance with her.

Pala. [*Aside.*] O Jupiter! What a blockhead was I, not to find it out! My wife, that must be, is his mistress. I did a little suspect it before. Well, I must marry her, because she's handsome, and because I hate to be disinherited by a younger brother, which I am sure I shall be, if I disobey; and yet I must keep in with Rhodophil, because I love his wife.
[*To* **Rhodophil.**]
I must desire you to make my excuse to your lady, if I have been so unfortunate to cause any mistake; and, withal, to beg the honour of being known to her.

Rhod. O, that is but reason. Hark you, spouse, pray look upon this gentleman as my friend; whom, to my knowledge, you have never seen before this hour.

Dora. I am so obedient a wife, sir, that my husband's commands shall ever be a law to me.

[*Enter* **Melantha** *again, hastily, and runs to embrace* **Doralice.**]

Mela. O, my dear, I was just going to pay my *devoirs* to you; I had not time this morning, for making my court to the king, and our new prince. Well, never nation was so happy, and all that, in a young prince; and he is the kindest person in the world to me, let me die if he is not.

Dora. He has been bred up far from court, and therefore —

Mela. That imports not: Though he has not seen the *grand monde,* and all that, let me die but he has the air of the court most absolutely.

Pala. But yet, madam, he —

Mela. O, servant, you can testify that I am in his good graces. Well, I cannot stay long with you, because I have promised him this afternoon to — But hark you, my dear, I'll tell you a secret.
[*Whispers to* **Doralice.**]

Rhod. [*Aside.*] The devil's in me, that I must love this woman.

Pala. [*Aside.*] The devil's in me, that I must marry this woman.

Mela. [*Raising her voice.*] So the prince and I — But you must make a secret of this, my dear; for I would not for the world your husband should hear it, or my tyrant, there, that must be.

Pala. [*Aside.*] Well, fair impertinent, your whisper is not lost, we hear you.

Dora. I understand then, that —

Mela. I'll tell you, my dear, the prince took me by the hand, and pressed it *à la derobbée,* because the king was near, made the *doux yeux* to me, and, *ensuite,* said a thousand gallantries, or let me die, my dear.

Dora. Then I am sure you —

Mela. You are mistaken, my dear.

Dora. What, before I speak?

Mela. But I know your meaning. You think, my dear, that I assumed something of *fierté* into my countenance, to rebute, him; but, quite contrary, I *regard*-ed him, — I know not how to express it in our dull Sicilian language, — *d'un air enjoüé;* and said nothing but *ad autre, ad autre,* and that it was all *grimace,* and would not pass upon me.
[*Enter* **Artemis**: *Melantha sees her, and runs away from* **Doralice.**]
[*To* **Artemis.**]

My dear, I must beg your pardon, I was just making a loose from Doralice, to pay my respects to you. Let me die, if I ever pass time so agreeably as in your company, and if I would leave it for any lady's in Sicily.

Arte. The princess Amalthea is coming this way.

[*Enter* **Amalthea**: **Melantha** *runs to her.*]

Mela. O, dear madam! I have been at your lodging in my new *galeche,* so often, to tell you of a new *amour,* betwixt two persons whom you would little suspect for it, that, let me die if one of my coach-horses be not dead, and another quite tired, and sunk under the *fatigue.*

Amal. O, Melantha, I can tell you news; the prince is coming this way.

Mela. The prince? O sweet prince! He and I are to — and I forgot it. — Your pardon, sweet madam, for my abruptness. —*Adieu,* my dear servant, — Rhodophil. — Servant, servant, servant all.

[*Exit running.*]

Amal. [*Whispers.*] Rhodophil, a word with you.

Dora. [*To* **Palamede**.] Why do you not follow your mistress, sir?

Pala. Follow her? Why, at this rate she'll be at the Indies within this half hour.

Dora. However, if you cannot follow her all day, you will meet her at night, I hope?

Pala. But can you, in charity, suffer me to be so mortified, without affording me some relief? If it be but to punish that sign of a husband there, that lazy matrimony, that dull insipid taste, who leaves such delicious fare at home, to dine abroad on worse meat, and pay dear for it into the bargain.

Dora. All this is in vain: Assure yourself, I will never admit of any visit from you in private.

Pala. That is to tell me, in other words, my condition is desperate.

Dora. I think you in so ill a condition, that I am resolved to pray for you, this very evening, in the close walk behind the terrace; for that's a private place, and there I am sure nobody will disturb my devotions. And so, good-night, sir.

[*Exit.*]

Pala. This is the newest way of making an appointment I ever heard of. Let women alone to contrive the means; I find we are but dunces to them. Well, I will not be so prophane a wretch as to interrupt her devotions; but, to make them more effectual, I'll down upon my knees, and endeavour to join my own with them.

[*Exit.*]

Amal. [*To* **Rhodophil.**] I know already they do not love each other; and that my brother acts but a forced obedience to the king's commands; so that if a quarrel should arise betwixt the prince and him, I were most miserable on both sides.

Rhod. There shall be nothing wanting in me, madam, to prevent so sad a consequence.
[*Enter* **King Polydamus** *and* **Leonidas**; *the* **King** *whispers to* **Amalthea**.]
[*To himself.*]
I begin to hate this Palamede, because he is to marry my mistress: Yet break with him I dare not, for fear of being quite excluded from her company. It is a hard case, when a man must go by his rival to his mistress: But it is, at worst, but using him like a pair of heavy boots in a dirty journey; after I have fouled him all day, I'll throw him off at night.

[*Exit.*]

Amal. [*To the* **King**.] This honour is too great for me to hope.

Poly. You shall this hour have the assurance of it.
Leonidas, come hither; you have heard,
I doubt not, that the father of this princess
Was my most faithful friend, while I was yet
A private man; and when I did assume
This crown, he served me in the high attempt.

You see, then, to what gratitude obliges me;
Make your addresses to her.

Leon. Sir, I am yet too young to be a courtier;
I should too much betray my ignorance,
And want of breeding to so fair a lady.

Amal. Your language speaks you not bred up in deserts,
But in the softness of some Asian court,
Where luxury and ease invent kind words,
To cozen tender virgins of their hearts.

Poly. You need not doubt,
But in what words soe'er a prince can offer
His crown and person, they will be received.
You know my pleasure, and you know your duty.

Leon. Yes, sir, I shall obey, in what I can.

Poly. In what you can, Leonidas? Consider,
He's both your king, and father, who commands you.
Besides, what is there hard in my injunction?

Leon. 'Tis hard to have my inclination forced.
I would not marry, sir; and, when I do,
I hope you'll give me freedom in my choice.

Poly. View well this lady,
Whose mind as much transcends her beauteous face,
          As that excels all others.

Amal. My beauty, as it ne'er could merit love,
So neither can it beg: And, sir, you may
Believe, that what the king has offered you,
I should refuse, did I not value more
Your person than your crown.

Leon.   Think it not pride,
Or my new fortunes swell me to contemn you;
Think less, that I want eyes to see your beauty;
And, least of all, think duty wanting in me
To obey a father's will: But —

Poly.   But what, Leonidas?

For I must know your reason; and be sure
It be convincing too.

Leon. Sir, ask the stars,
Which have imposed love on us, like a fate,
Why minds are bent to one, and fly another?
Ask, why all beauties cannot move all hearts?
For though there may be made a rule for colour,
Or for feature, there can be none for liking.

Poly. Leonidas, you owe me more
Than to oppose your liking to my pleasure.

Leon. I owe you all things, sir; but something, too,
I owe myself.

Poly. You shall dispute no more; I am a king,
           And I will be obeyed.

Leon. You are a king, sir, but you are no god;
Or, if you were, you could not force my will.

Poly. [*Aside.*] But you are just, ye gods; O you are just,
In punishing the crimes of my rebellion
With a rebellious son! Yet I can punish him, as you do me.
Leonidas, there is no jesting with
My will: I ne'er had done so much to gain
A crown, but to be absolute in all things.

Amal. O, sir, be not so much a king, as to
Forget you are a father: Soft indulgence
Becomes that name. Tho' nature gives you power
To bind his duty, 'tis with silken bonds:
Command him, then, as you command yourself;
He is as much a part of you, as are
Your appetite and will, and those you force not,
But gently bend, and make them pliant to your reason.

Poly. It may be I have used too rough a way —
Forgive me, my Leonidas; I know
I lie as open to the gusts of passion,
As the bare shore to every, beating surge:
I will not force thee now; but I entreat thee,
Absolve a father's vow to this fair virgin;
A vow, which hopes of having such a son

First caused.

Leon. Show not my disobedience by your prayers;
For I must still deny you, though I now
Appear more guilty to myself than you:
I have some reasons, which I cannot utter,
That force my disobedience; yet I mourn
To death, that the first thing, you e'er enjoined me,
Should be that only one command in nature,
         Which I could not obey.

Poly. I did descend too much below myself,
When I entreated him. — Hence, to thy desert!
Thou'rt not my son, or art not fit to be.

Amal. [*Kneeling.*] Great sir, I humbly beg you, make not me
The cause of your displeasure. I absolve
Your vow; far from me be such designs;
So wretched a desire of being great,
By making him unhappy. You may see
Something so noble in the prince's nature,
As grieves him more, not to obey, than you,
That you are not obeyed.

Poly.   Then, for your sake,
I'll give him one day longer to consider,
Not to deny; for my resolves are firm
As fate, that cannot change.

        [*Exeunt* **Polydamus** *and* **Amalthea**.]

Leon.   And so are mine.
This beauteous princess, charming as she is,
Could never make me happy: I must first
Be false to my Palmyra, and then wretched.
But, then, a father's anger! Suppose he should
Recede from his own vow, he never would
Permit me to keep mine.
         [*Enter* **Palmyra**; **Argaleon** *following her, a little after.*]
         See, she appears!
I'll think no more of any thing, but her.
Yet I have one good hour ere I am wretched.
But, oh! Argaleon follows her! So night
Treads on the footsteps of a winter's sun,
And stalks all black behind him.

Palm.   O, Leonidas,
For I must call you still by that dear name,
Free me from this bad man.

Leon. I hope he dares not be injurious to you.

Arga. I rather was injurious to myself,
Than her.

Leon. That must be judged, when I hear what you said.

Arga. I think you need not give yourself that trouble:
     It concerned us alone.

Leon. You answer saucily, and indirectly:
What interest can you pretend in her?

Arga. It may be, sir, I made her some expressions
Which I would not repeat, because they were
Below my rank, to one of hers.

Leon.   What did he say, Palmyra?

Palm. I'll tell you all: First, he began to look,
And then he sighed, and then he looked again;
At last, he said, my eyes wounded his heart:
And, after that, he talked of flames and fires,
And such strange words, that I believed he conjured.

Leon. O my heart! Leave me, Argaleon.

Arga. Come, sweet Palmyra,
I will instruct you better in my meaning:
You see he would be private.

Leon.   Go yourself,
And leave her here.

Arga.   Alas, she's ignorant,
And is not fit to entertain a prince.

Leon. First learn what's fit for you; that's to obey.

Arga. I know my duty is to wait on you.
A great king's son, like you, ought to forget
Such mean converse.

Leon.   What? a disputing subject?
Hence, or my sword shall do me justice on thee.

Arga. [*Going.*] Yet I may find a time —

Leon. [*Going after him.*] What's that you mutter,
To find a time? —

Arga.   To wait on you again —
            [*Softly.*]
In the mean while I'll watch you.
            [*Exit, and watches during the scene.*]

Leon. How precious are the hours of love in courts!
In cottages, where love has all the day,
Full, and at ease, he throws it half away.
Time gives himself, and is not valued, there;
But sells at mighty rates, each minute, here:
There, he is lazy, unemployed, and slow;
Here, he's more swift; and yet has more to do.
So many of his hours in public move,
That few are left for privacy and love.

Palm. The sun, methinks, shines faint and dimly, here;
Light is not half so long, nor half so clear:
But, oh! When every day was yours and mine,
How early up! What haste he made to shine!

Leon. Such golden days no prince must hope to see,
Whose every subject is more bless'd than he.

Palm. Do you remember, when their tasks were done,
How all the youth did to our cottage run?
While winter-winds were whistling loud without,
Our cheerful hearth was circled round about:
With strokes in ashes, maids their lovers drew;
And still you fell to me, and I to you.

Leon. When love did of my heart possession take,
I was so young, my soul was scarce awake:

I cannot tell when first I thought you fair;
But sucked in love, insensibly as air.

Palm. I know too well when, first my love began,
When at our wake you for the chaplet ran:
Then I was made the lady of the May,
And, with the garland, at the goal did stay:
Still, as you ran, I kept you full in view;
I hoped, and wished, and ran, methought, for you.
As you came near, I hastily did rise,
And stretched my arm outright, that held the prize.
The custom was to kiss whom I should crown;
You kneeled, and in my lap your head laid down:
I blushed, and blushed, and did the kiss delay;
At last my subjects forced me to obey:
But, when I gave the crown, and then the kiss,
I scarce had breath to say, "Take that, — and this."

Leon. I felt, the while, a pleasing kind of smart;
That kiss went, tingling, to my very heart.
When it was gone, the sense of it did stay;
The sweetness clinged upon my lips all day,
Like drops of honey, loath to fall away.

Palm. Life, like a prodigal, gave all his store
To my first youth, and now can give no more.
You are a prince; and, in that high degree,
No longer must converse with humble me.

Leon. 'Twas to my loss the gods that title gave;
A tyrant's son is doubly born a slave:
He gives a crown; but, to prevent my life
From being happy, loads it with a wife.

Palm. Speak quickly; what have you resolved to do?

Leon. To keep my faith inviolate to you.
He threatens me with exile, and with shame,
To lose my birthright, and a prince's name;
But there's a blessing which he did not mean,
To send me back to love and you again.

Palm. Why was not I a princess for your sake?
But heav'n no more such miracles can make:
And, since that cannot, this must never be;

You shall not lose a crown for love of me.
Live happy, and a nobler choice pursue;
I shall complain of fate, but not of you.

Leon. Can you so easily without me live?
Or could you take the counsel, which you give?
Were you a princess, would you not be true?

Palm. I would; but cannot merit it from you.

Leon. Did you not merit, as you do, my heart,
Love gives esteem, and then it gives desert.
But if I basely could forget my vow,
Poor helpless innocence, what would you do?

Palm. In woods, and plains, where first my love began,
There would I live, retired from faithless man:
I'd sit all day within some lonely shade,
Or that close arbour which your hands have made:
I'd search the groves, and every tree, to find
Where you had carved our names upon the rind:
Your hook, your scrip, all that was yours, I'd keep,
And lay them by me when I went to sleep.
Thus would I live: And maidens, when I die,
Upon my hearse white true-love-knots should tie;
And thus my tomb should be inscribed above,
Here the forsaken Virgin rests from love.

Leon. Think not that time or fate shall e'er divide
Those hearts, which love and mutual vows have tied.
But we must part; farewell, my love.

Palm.   Till when?

Leon. Till the next age of hours we meet again.
Meantime, we may,
When near each other we in public stand,
Contrive to catch a look, or steal a hand:
Fancy will every touch and glance improve;
And draw the most spirituous parts of love.
Our souls sit close, and silently within,
And their own web from their own entrails spin;
And when eyes meet far off, our sense is such,
That, spider-like, we feel the tenderest touch.

[*Exeunt.*]

ACT III.
SCENE I.

[Enter **Rhodophil**, *meeting* **Doralice** *and* **Artemis**; **Rhodophil** *and* **Doralice** *embrace.]*

Rhod. My own dear heart!

Dora. My own true love!
   [She starts back.]
I had forgot myself to be so kind; indeed, I am very angry with you, dear; you are come home an hour after you appointed: if you had stayed a minute longer, I was just considering whether I should stab, hang, or drown myself.
   [Embracing him.]

Rhod. Nothing but the king's business could have hindered me; and I was so vexed, that I was just laying down my commission, rather than have failed my dear.
   [Kisses her hand.]

Arte. Why, this is love as it should be betwixt man and wife: such another couple would bring marriage into fashion again. But is it always thus betwixt you?

Rhod. Always thus! This is nothing. I tell you, there is not such a pair of turtles in Sicily; there is such an eternal cooing and kissing betwixt us, that indeed it is scandalous before civil company.

Dora. Well, if I had imagined I should have been this fond fool, I would never have married the man I loved: I married to be happy, and have made myself miserable by over-loving. Nay, and now my case is desperate; for I have been married above these two years, and find myself every day worse and worse in love: nothing but madness can be the end on't.

Arte. Dote on, to the extremity, and you are happy.

Dora. He deserves so infinitely much, that, the truth is, there can be no doting in the matter; but, to love well, I confess, is a work that pays itself: 'Tis telling gold, and, after, taking it for one's pains.

Rhod. By that I should be a very covetous person; for I am ever pulling out my money, and putting it into my pocket again.

Dora. O dear Rhodophil!

Rhod. [*Embracing each other.*] O sweet Doralice!

Arte. [*Aside.*] Nay, I am resolved, I'll never interrupt lovers: I'll leave them as happy as I found them.
[*Steals away.*]

Rhod. [*Looking up.*] What, is she gone?

Dora. Yes; and without taking leave.

Rhod. Then there's enough for this time.
[*Parting from her.*]

Dora. Yes, sure, the scene is done, I take it.

[*They walk contrary ways on the stage; he, with his hands in his pockets, whistling; she singing a dull melancholy tune.*]

Rhod. Pox o' your dull tune, a man can't think for you.

Dora. Pox o' your damned whistling; you can neither be company to me yourself, nor leave me to the freedom of my own fancy.

Rhod. Well, thou art the most provoking wife!

Dora. Well, thou art the dullest husband, thou art never to be provoked.

Rhod. I was never thought dull till I married thee; and now thou hast made an old knife of me; thou hast whetted me so long, till I have no edge left.

Dora. I see you are in the husband's fashion; you reserve all your good humours for your mistresses, and keep your ill for your wives.

Rhod. Prythee leave me to my own cogitations; I am thinking over all my sins, to find for which of them it was I married thee.

Dora. Whatever your sin was, mine's the punishment.

Rhod. My comfort is, thou art not immortal; and, when that blessed, that divine day comes of thy departure, I'm resolved I'll make one holiday more in the almanack for thy sake.

Dora. Ay, you had need make a holiday for me, for I am sure you have made me a martyr.

Rhod. Then, setting my victorious foot upon thy head, in the first hour of thy silence, (that is, the first hour thou art dead, for I despair of it before) I will swear by thy ghost — an oath as terrible to me as Styx is to the gods — never more to be in danger of the banes of matrimony.

Dora. And I am resolved to marry the very same day thou diest, if it be but to show how little I'm concerned for thee.

Rhod. Pray thee, Doralice, why do we quarrel thus a-days? Ha! This is but a kind of heathenish life, and does not answer the ends of marriage. If I have erred, propound what reasonable atonement may be made before we sleep, and I will not be refractory; but withal consider, I have been married these three years, and be not too tyrannical.

Dora. What should you talk of a peace a-bed, when you can give no security for performance of articles?

Rhod. Then, since we must live together, and both of us stand upon our terms, as to matters of dying first, let us make ourselves as merry as we can with our misfortunes. Why, there's the devil on't! If thou could'st make my enjoying thee but a little easy, or a little more unlawful, thou should'st see what a termagant lover I would prove. I have taken such pains to enjoy thee, Doralice, that I have fancied thee all the fine women of the town — to help me out: But now there's none left for me to think on, my imagination is quite jaded. Thou art a wife, and thou wilt be a wife, and I can make thee another no longer.

[*Exit* **Rhodophil**.]

Dora. Well, since thou art a husband, and wilt be a husband, I'll try if I can find out another. 'Tis a pretty time we women have on't, to be made widows while we are married. Our husbands think it reasonable to complain, that we are the same, and the same to them, when we have more reason to complain, that they are not the same to us. Because they cannot feed on one dish, therefore we must be starved. 'Tis enough that they have a sufficient ordinary provided, and a table ready spread for them: If they cannot fall too, and eat heartily, the fault is theirs; and 'tis pity, methinks, that the good creature should be lost, when many a poor sinner would be glad on't.

[*Enter* **Melantha** *and* **Artemis** *to her.*]

Mela. Dear, my dear, pity me, I am so *chagrin* today, and have had the most signal *affront* at court! I went this afternoon to do my *devoir* to princess Amalthea, found her, conversed with her, and helped to make her court some half an hour; after which, she went to take the air, chose out two ladies to go with her, that came in after me, and left me most barbarously behind her.

Arte. You are the less to be pitied, Melantha, because you subject yourself to these affronts, by coming perpetually to court, where you have no business nor employment.

Mela. I declare, I had rather of the two be rallied nay, *mal traitée* at court, than be deified in the town; for, assuredly, nothing can be so *ridicule* as a mere town lady.

Dora. Especially at court. How I have seen them crowd and sweat in the drawing-room on a holiday-night! For that's their time to swarm and invade the presence. O, how they catch at a bow, or any little salute from a courtier, to make show of their acquaintance! And, rather than be thought to be quite unknown, they court'sy to one another; but they take true pains to come near the circle, and press and peep upon the princess, to write letters into the country how she was dressed, while the ladies, that stand about, make their court to her with abusing them.

Arte. These are sad truths, Melantha; and therefore I would e'en advise you to quit the court, and live either wholly in the town, or, if you like not that, in the country.

Dora. In the country! Nay, that's to fall beneath the town, for they live upon our offals here. Their entertainment of wit is only the remembrance of what they had when they were last in town; they live this year upon the last year's knowledge, as their cattle do all night, by chewing the cud of what they eat in the afternoon.

Mela. And they tell, for news, such unlikely stories! A letter from one of us is such a present to them, that the poor souls wait for the carrier's-day with such devotion, that they cannot sleep the night before.

Arte. No more than I can, the night before I am to go a journey.

Dora. Or I, before I am to try on a new gown.

Mela. A song, that's stale here, will be new there a twelvemonth hence; and if a man of the town by chance come amongst them, he's reverenced for teaching them the tune.

Dora. A friend of mine, who makes songs sometimes, came lately out of the west, and vowed he was so put out of countenance with a song of his; for, at the first country gentleman's he visited, he saw three tailors cross legged upon the table in the hall, who were tearing out as loud as ever they could sing:
  — *After the pangs of a desperate lover, &c.*
And that all day he heard of nothing else, but the daughters of the house, and the maids, humming it over in every corner, and the father whistling it.

Arte. Indeed, I have observed of myself, that when I am out of town but a fortnight, I am so humble, that I would receive a letter from my tailor or mercer for a favour.

Mela. When I have been at grass in the summer, and am new come up again, methinks I'm to be turned into ridicule by all that see me; but when I have been once or twice at court, I begin to value myself again, and to despise my country acquaintance.

Arte. There are places where all people may be adored, and we ought to know ourselves so well as to choose them.

Dora. That's very true; your little courtier's wife, who speaks to the king but once a month, need but go to a town lady, and there she may vapour and cry, "The king and I," at every word. Your town lady, who is laughed at in the circle, takes her coach into the city, and there she's called Your honour, and has a banquet from the merchant's wife, whom she laughs at for her kindness. And, as for my finical cit, she removes but to her country house, and there insults over the country gentlewoman that never comes up, who treats her with furmity and custard, and opens her dear bottle of mirabilis beside, for a gill-glass of it at parting.

Arte. At last, I see, we shall leave Melantha where we found her; for, by your description of the town and country, they are become more dreadful to her than the court, where she was affronted. But you forget we are to wait on the princess Amalthea. Come, Doralice.

Dora. Farewell, Melantha.

Mela. Adieu, my dear.

Arte. You are out of charity with her, and therefore I shall not give your service.

Mela. Do not omit it, I beseech you; for I have such a *tendre* for the court, that I love it even from the drawing-room to the lobby, and can never be *rebutée* by any usage. But hark you, my dears; one thing I had forgot, of great concernment.

Dora. Quickly then, we are in haste.

Mela. Do not call it my service, that's too vulgar; but do my *baise mains* to the princess Amalthea; that is *spirituelle*!

Dora. To do you service, then, we will *prendre* the *carosse* to court, and do your *baise mains* to the princess Amalthea, in your phrase *spirituelle*.

[*Exeunt* **Artemis** *and* **Doralice**.]
[*Enter* **Philotis**, *with a paper in her hand.*]

Mela. O, are you there, *mignon*? And, well, are not you a most precious damsel, to *retard* all my visits for want of *language*, when you know you are paid so well for furnishing me with new words for my daily conversation? Let me die, if I have not run the *risque* already to speak like one of the vulgar, and if I have one phrase left in all my store, that is not thread-bare *et usé*, and fit for nothing but to be thrown to peasants.

Phil. Indeed, Madam, I have been very diligent in my vocation; but you have so drained all the French plays and romances, that they are not able to supply you with words for your daily expence.

Mela. Drained? What a word's there! *Epuisée,* you sot you. Come, produce your morning's work.

Phil. 'Tis here, madam.
              [*Shows the paper.*]

Mela. O, my Venus! Fourteen or fifteen words to serve me a whole day! Let me die, at this rate I cannot last till night. Come, read your works: Twenty to one, half of them will not pass muster neither.

Phil. [*Reads.*] *Sottises.*

Mela. Sottises: bon. That's an excellent word to begin withal; as, for example, he or she said a thousand *sottises* to me. Proceed.

Phil. Figure: As, what a *figure* of a man is there! *Naive,* and *naiveté.*

Mela. Naive! as how?

Phil. Speaking of a thing that was naturally said, it was so *naive;* or, such an innocent piece of simplicity 'twas such a *naiveté.*

Mela. Truce with your interpretations. Make haste.

Phil. Foible, chagrin, grimace, embarrasse, double entendre, equivoque, ecclaircissement, suittè, beveue, façon, penchant, coup d'etourdy, and *ridicule.*

Mela. Hold, hold; how did they begin?

Phil. They began at *sottises,* and ended *en ridicule.*

Mela. Now, give me your paper in my hand, and hold you my glass, while I practice my *postures* for the day.
              [**Melantha** *laughs in the glass.*]
How does that laugh become my face?

Phil. Sovereignly well, madam.

Mela. Sovereignly? Let me die, that's not amiss. That word shall not be yours; I'll invent it, and bring it up myself: My new *point gorget* shall be yours upon't. Not a word of the word, I charge you.

Phil. I am dumb, madam.

Mela. [*Looking in the glass again.*] That glance, how suits it with my face?

Phil. 'Tis so *languissant*!

Mela. Languissant! That word shall be mine too, and my last Indian gown thine for't. That sigh?
 [*Looks again.*]

Phil. 'Twill make a man sigh, madam. 'Tis a mere *incendiary*.

Mela. Take my guimp petticoat for that truth. If thou hast most of these phrases, let me die but I could give away all my wardrobe, and go naked for them.

Phil. Go naked? Then you would be a Venus, madam. O Jupiter! What had I forgot? This paper was given me by Rhodophil's page.

Mela. [*Reading the letter.*] Beg the favour from you... Gratify my passion... so far... assignation... in the grotto... behind the terrace — clock this evening — Well, for the *billets doux* there is no man in Sicily must dispute with Rhodophil; they are so French, so gallant, and so *tendre*, that I cannot resist the temptation of the assignation. Now, go you away, Philotis; it imports me to practice what to say to my servant when I meet him.
 [*Exit* **Philotis**.]
"Rhodophil, you'll wonder at my assurance to meet you here; let me die, I am so out of breath with coming, that I can render you no reason of it." Then he will make this *repartee*; "Madam, I have no reason to accuse you for that which is so great a favour to me." Then I reply, "But why have you drawn me to this solitary place? Let me die, but I am apprehensive of some violence from you." Then says he, "Solitude, madam, is most fit for lovers; but by this fair hand — " "Nay, now I vow you're rude, sir. O fy, fy, fy; I hope you'll be honourable?" — "You'd laugh at me if I should, madam." "What, do you mean to throw me down thus? Ah me! ah! ah! ah!"

[*Enter* **Polydamas, Leonidas,** *and* **Guards.**]
O Venus! The king and court. Let me die, but I fear they have found my *foible*, and will turn me into *ridicule*.
[*Exit, running.*]

Leon. Sir, I beseech you.

Poly. Do not urge my patience.

Leon. I'll not deny,
But what your spies informed you of is true:
I love the fair Palmyra; but I loved her
Before I knew your title to my blood.
[*Enter* **Palmyra** *guarded.*]
See, here she comes, and looks, amidst her guards,
Like a weak dove under the falcon's gripe.
O heaven, I cannot bear it.

Poly. Maid, come hither.
Have you presumed so far, as to receive
My son's affections?

Palm. Alas, what shall I answer? To confess it
Will raise a blush upon a virgin's face;
Yet I was ever taught 'twas base to lie.

Poly. You've been too bold, and you must love no more.

Palm. Indeed I must; I cannot help my love;
I was so tender when I took the bent,
That now I grow that way.

Poly. He is a prince, and you are meanly born.

Leon. Love either finds equality, or makes it:
Like death, he knows no difference in degrees,
But plains, and levels all.

Palm. Alas! I had not rendered up my heart,
Had he not loved me first; but he preferred me
Above the maidens of my age and rank,
— Still shunned their company, and still sought mine.
I was not won by gifts, yet still he gave;
And all his gifts, though small, yet spoke his love.

He picked the earliest strawberries in woods,
The clustered filberds, and the purple grapes;
He taught a prating stare to speak my name;
And, when he found a nest of nightingales,
Or callow linnets, he would show them me,
And let me take them out.

Poly. This is a little mistress, meanly born,
Fit only for a prince's vacant hours,
And then, to laugh at her simplicity,
Not fix a passion there. Now hear my sentence.

Leon. Remember, ere you give it, 'tis pronounced
Against us both.

Poly.   First, in her hand
There shall be placed a player's painted sceptre,
And, on her head, a gilded pageant crown:
Thus shall she go,
With all the boys attending on her triumph;
That done, be put alone into a boat,
With bread and water only for three days;
So on the sea she shall be set adrift,
And who relieves her dies.

Palm. I only beg that you would execute
The last part first: Let me be put to sea;
The bread and water for my three days life
I give you back, I would not live so long;
But let me 'scape the shame.

Leon. Look to me, piety; and you, O Gods, look to my piety!
Keep me from saying that, which misbecomes a son;
But let me die before I see this done.

Poly. If you for ever will abjure her sight,
I can be yet a father; she shall live.

Leon. Hear, O you powers! Is this to be a father?
I see 'tis all my happiness and quiet
You aim at, sir; and take them:
I will not save even my Palmyra's life
At that ignoble price; but I'll die with her.

Palm. So had I done by you, had fate made me a princess.

Death, methinks, is not a terror now:
He is not fierce, or grim, but fawns, and sooths me,
And slides along, like Cleopatra's aspick,
Offering his service to my troubled breast.

Leon. Begin what you have purposed when you please;
Lead her to scorn, your triumph shall be doubled.
As holy priests, in pity, go with dying malefactors,
So I will share her shame.

Poly. You shall not have your will so much;
First part them, then execute your office.

Leon.   No; I'll die in her defence.
               [*Draws his sword.*]

Palm. Ah, hold, and pull not on
A curse, to make me worthy of my death:
Do not by lawless force oppose your father,
Whom you have too much disobeyed for me.

Leon. Here, take it, sir, and with it pierce my heart:
      [*Presenting his sword to his Father upon his knees.*]
You have done more in taking my Palmyra.
You are my father; therefore I submit.

Poly. Keep him from any thing he may design
Against his life, while the first fury lasts;
And now perform what I commanded you.

Leon. In vain; if sword and poison be denied me,
I'll hold my breath and die.

Palm. Farewell, my last Leonidas; yet live,
I charge you, live, 'till you believe me dead.
I cannot die in peace, if you die first;
If life's a blessing, you shall have it last.

Poly. Go on with her, and lead him after me.

      [*Enter* **Argaleon** *hastily, with* **Hermogenes**.]

Arga. I bring you, sir, such news as must amaze you,
And such as will prevent you from an action,

Which would have rendered all your life unhappy.

[**Hermogenes** *kneels.*]

Poly. Hermogenes, you bend your knees in vain,
My doom's already past.

Herm. I kneel not for Palmyra, for I know
She will not need my prayers; but for myself:
With a feigned tale I have abused your ears,
And, therefore, merit death: but since, unforced,
I first accuse myself, I hope your mercy.

Poly. Haste to explain your meaning.

Herm. Then, in few words, Palmyra is your daughter.

Poly. How can I give belief to this impostor?
He, who has once abused me, often may.
I'll hear no more.

Arga. For your own sake, you must.

Herm. A parent's love — for I confess my crime —
Moved me to say, Leonidas was yours;
But when I heard Palmyra was to die,
The fear of guiltless blood so stung my conscience,
That I resolved, even with my shame,
To save your daughter's life.

Poly. But how can I be certain, but that interest,
Which moved you first to say your son was mine,
Does not now move you too, to save your daughter?

Herm. You had but then my word; I bring you now
Authentic testimonies. Sir, in short,
        [*Delivers on his knees a jewel, and letter.*]
If this will not convince you, let me suffer.

Poly. I know this jewel well; 'twas once my mother's,
        [*Looking first on the jewel.*]
Which, marrying, I presented to my wife.
And this, O this is my Eudocia's hand:
        [*Reads.*]

This was the pledge of love given to Eudocia,
Who, dying, to her young Palmyra leaves it;
And this, when you, my dearest lord, receive,
Own her, and think on me, dying Eudocia.
           [*To* **Argaleon**.]
Take it; 'tis well there is no more to read.
My eyes grow full, and swim in their own light.
           [*He embraces* **Palmyra**.]

Palm. I fear, sir, this is your intended pageant.
You sport yourself at poor Palmyra's cost;
But if you think to make me proud,
Indeed I cannot be so: I was born
With humble thoughts, and lowly, like my birth.
A real fortune could not make me haughty,
Much less a feigned.

Poly. This was her mother's temper.
I have too much deserved thou shouldst suspect
That I am not thy father; but my love
Shall henceforth show I am. Behold my eyes,
And see a father there begin to flow:
This is not feigned, Palmyra.

Palm. I doubt no longer, sir; you are a king,
And cannot lie: Falsehood's a vice too base
To find a room in any royal breast.
I know, in spite of my unworthiness,
I am your child; for when you would have killed me,
Methought I loved you then.

Arga. Sir, we forget the prince Leonidas;
His greatness should not stand neglected thus.

Poly. Guards, you may now retire;
Give him his sword, and leave him free.

Leon. Then the first use I make of liberty
Shall be, with your permission, mighty sir,
To pay that reverence to which nature binds me.
           [*Kneels to* **Hermogenes**.]

Arga. Sure you forget your birth, thus to misplace
This act of your obedience; you should kneel
To nothing but to heaven, and to a king.

Leon. I never shall forget what nature owes,
Nor be ashamed to pay it; though my father
Be not a king, I know him brave and honest,
And well deserving of a worthier son.

Poly. He bears it gallantly.

Leon. [*To* **Hermogenes**.]   Why would you not instruct me,
Sir, before,where I should place my duty?
From which, if ignorance have made me swerve,
I beg your pardon for an erring son.

Palm. I almost grieve I am a princess, since
It makes him lose a crown.

Leon. And next, to you, my king, thus low I kneel,
To implore your mercy; if in that small time
I had the honour to be thought your son,
I paid not strict obedience to your will.
I thought, indeed, I should not be compelled,
But thought it as your son; so what I took
In duty from you, I restored in courage;
Because your son should not be forced.

Poly. You have my pardon for it.

Leon. To you, fair princess, I congratulate
Your birth; of which I ever thought you worthy:
And give me leave to add, that I am proud
The gods have picked me out to be the man,
By whose dejected fate yours is to rise;
Because no man could more desire your fortune,
Or franklier part with his, to make you great.

Palm. I know the king, though you are not his son,
Will still regard you as my foster-brother,
And so conduct you downward from a throne,
By slow degrees, so unperceived and soft,
That it may seem no fall: Or, if it be,
May fortune lay a bed of down beneath you!

Poly. He shall be ranked with my nobility,
And kept from scorn by a large pension given him.

Leon. [*Bowing.*] You are all great and royal in your gifts;
But at the donor's feet I lay them down:
Should I take riches from you, it would seem
As I did want a soul to bear that poverty,
To which the gods designed my humble birth:
And should I take your honours without merit,
It would appear, I wanted manly courage
To hope them, in your service, from my sword.

Poly. Still brave, and like yourself.
The court shall shine this night in its full splendour,
And celebrate this new discovery.
Argaleon, lead my daughter: As we go,
I shall have time to give her my commands,
              In which you are concerned.

[*Exeunt all but* **Leonidas.**]

Leon. Methinks, I do not want
That huge long train of fawning followers,
That swept a furlong after me. 'Tis true I am alone;
So was the godhead, ere he made the world,
And better served himself, than served by nature.
              And yet I have a soul
Above this humble fate. I could command,
Love to do good, give largely to true merit,
All that a king should do: But though these are not
My province, I have scene enough within,
To exercise my virtue.
All that a heart, so fixed as mine, can move,
Is, that my niggard fortune starves my love.

[*Exit.*]

SCENE II.

[**Palamede** *and* **Doralice** *meet: She, with a book in her hand, seems to start at the sight of him.*]

Dora. 'Tis a strange thing that no warning will serve your turn; and that no retirement will secure me from your impertinent addresses! Did not I tell you, that I was to be private here at my devotions?

Pala. Yes; and you see I have observed my cue exactly: I am come to relieve you from them. Come, shut up, shut up your book; the man's come who is to supply all your necessities.

Dora. Then, it seems, you are so impudent to think it was an assignation? This, I warrant, was your lewd interpretation of my innocent meaning.

Pala. Venus forbid, that I should harbour so unreasonable a thought of a fair young lady, that you should lead me hither into temptation. I confess, I might think indeed it was a kind of honourable challenge, to meet privately without seconds, and decide the difference betwixt the two sexes; but heaven forgive me, if I thought amiss.

Dora. You thought too, I'll lay my life on't, that you might as well make love to me, as my husband does to your mistress.

Pala. I was so unreasonable to think so too.

Dora. And then you wickedly inferred, that there was some justice in the revenge of it; or, at least, but little injury for a man to endeavour to enjoy that, which he accounts a blessing, and which is not valued as it ought by the dull possessor. Confess your wickedness — did you not think so?

Pala. I confess I was thinking so, as fast as I could; but you think so much before me, that you will let me think nothing.

Dora. 'Tis the very thing that I designed; I have forestalled all your arguments, and left you without a word more, to plead for mercy. If you have any thing farther to offer, ere sentence pass — Poor animal, I brought you hither only for my diversion.

Pala. That you may have, if you'll make use of me the right way; but I tell thee, woman, I am now past talking.

Dora. But it may be, I came hither to hear what fine things you could say for yourself.

Pala. You would be very angry, to my knowledge, if I should lose so much time to say many of them. By this hand you would!

Dora. Fy, Palamede, I am a woman of honour.

Pala. I see you are; you have kept touch with your assignation: And before we part, you shall find that I am a man of honour. Yet I have one scruple of conscience —

Dora. I warrant you will not want some naughty argument, or other, to satisfy yourself. I hope you are afraid of betraying your friend?

Pala. Of betraying my friend! I am more afraid of being betrayed by you to my friend. You women now are got into the way of telling first yourselves: A man, who has any care of his reputation, will be loath to trust it with you.

Dora. O, you charge your faults upon our sex! You men are like cocks; you never make love, but you clap your wings, and crow when you have done.

Pala. Nay, rather you women are like hens; you never lay, but you cackle an hour after, to discover your nest. — But I'll venture it for once.

Dora. To convince you that you are in the wrong, I'll retire into the dark grotto, to my devotion, and make so little noise, that it shall be impossible for you to find me.

Pala. But if I find you —

Dora. Ay, if you find me — But I'll put you to search in more corners than you imagine.

[*She runs in, and he after her.*]

[Enter **Rhodophil** *and* **Melantha**.*]*

Mela. Let me die, but this solitude, and that grotto are scandalous; I'll go no further; besides, you have a sweet lady of your own.

Rhod. But a sweet mistress, now and then, makes my sweet lady so much more sweet.

Mela. I hope you will not force me?

Rhod. But I will, if you desire it.

Pala. [*Within.*] Where the devil are you, madam? 'Sdeath, I begin to be weary of this hide and seek: If you stay a little longer, till the fit's over, I'll hide in my turn, and put you to the finding me.
[*He enters, and sees* **Rhodophil** *and* **Melantha**.]
How! Rhodophil and my mistress!

Mela. My servant, to *apprehend* me! This is *surprenant au dernier*.

Rhod. I must on; there's nothing but impudence can help me out.

Pala. Rhodophil, how came you hither in so good company?

Rhod. As you see, Palamede; an effect of pure friendship; I was not able to live without you.

Pala. But what makes my mistress with you?

Rhod. Why, I heard you were here alone, and could not in civility but bring her to you.

Mela. You'll pardon the effects of a *passion* which I may now avow for you, if it transported me beyond the rules of *bienseance*.

Pala. But, who told you I was here? They, that told you that, may tell you more, for aught I know.

Rhod. O, for that matter, we had intelligence.

Pala. But let me tell you, we came hither so very privately, that you could not trace us.

Rhod. Us! What us? You are alone.

Pala. Us! The devil's in me for mistaking: — me, I meant. Or us, that is, you are me, or I you, as we are friends: That's us.

Dora. [*Within.*] Palamede, Palamede!

Rhod. I should know that voice; who's within there, that calls you?

Pala. Faith, I can't imagine; I believe the place is haunted.

Dora. [*Within.*] Palamede, Palamede, all-cocks hidden.

Pala. Lord, Lord, what shall I do? — Well, dear friend, to let you see I scorn to be jealous, and that I dare trust my mistress with you, take her back, for I would not willingly have her frighted, and I am resolved to see who's there; I'll not be daunted with a bugbear, that's certain: Prithee, dispute it not, it shall be so; nay do not put me to swear, but go quickly: There's an effort of pure friendship for you now.

[*Enter* **Doralice**, *and looks amazed, seeing them.*]

Rhod. Doralice! I am thunder-struck to see you here.

Pala. So am I! Quite thunder-struck. Was it you, that called me within? — I must be impudent.

Rhod. How came you hither, spouse?

Pala. Ay, how came you hither? And, which is more, how could you be here without my knowledge?

Dora. [*To her husband.*] O, gentlemen, have I caught you i'faith! Have I broke forth in ambush upon you! I thought my suspicions would prove true.

Rhod. Suspicions! This is very fine, spouse! Prithee, what suspicions?

Dora. O, you feign ignorance: Why, of you and Melantha; here have I stayed these two hours, waiting with all the rage of a passionate, loving wife, but infinitely jealous, to take you two in the manner; for hither I was certain you would come.

Rhod. But you are mistaken, spouse, in the occasion; for we came hither on purpose to find Palamede, on intelligence he was gone before.

Pala. I'll be hanged then, if the same party, who gave you intelligence I was here, did not tell your wife you would come hither. Now I smell the malice on't on both sides.

Dora. Was it so, think you? Nay, then, I'll confess my part of the malice too. As soon as ever I spied my husband and Melantha come together, I had a strange temptation to make him jealous in revenge; and that made me call Palamede, Palamede! As though there had been an intrigue between us.

Mela. Nay, I avow, there was an appearance of an intrigue between us too.

Pala. To see how things will come about!

Rhod. [*Embrace.*]And was it only thus, my dear Doralice?

Dora. [*Embracing him.*] And did I wrong n'own Rhodophil, with a false suspicion?

Pala. [*Aside.*] Now I am confident we had all four the same design: 'Tis a pretty odd kind of game this, where each of us plays for double stakes: This is just thrust and parry with the same motion; I am to get his wife, and yet to guard my own mistress. But I am vilely suspicious, that, while I conquer in the right wing, I shall be routed in the left; for both our women will certainly betray their party, because they are each of them for gaining of two, as well as we; and I much fear.
If their necessities and ours were known,
They have more need of two, than we of one.
    [*Exeunt, embracing one another.*]

ACT IV.
SCENE I.

[*Enter* **Leonidas**, *musing;* **Amalthea**, *following him.*]

Amal. Yonder he is; and I must speak or die;
And yet 'tis death to speak: yet he must know
I have a passion for him, and may know it
With a less blush; because to offer it
To his low fortunes, shows I loved before,
His person, not his greatness.

Leon. First scorned, and now commanded from the court!
The king is good; but he is wrought to this
By proud Argaleon's malice. What more
Disgrace can love and fortune join
To inflict upon one man? I cannot now
Behold my dear Palmyra: She, perhaps,
Too, is grown ashamed of a mean ill-placed love.

Amal. [*Aside.*] Assist me, Venus, for I tremble when
I am to speak, but I must force myself. —
Sir, I would crave but one short minute with you,
And some few words.

Leon. [*Aside.*] The proud Argaleon's sister!

Amal. [*Aside.*] Alas! It will not out; Shame stops my mouth. —
Pardon my error, sir; I was mistaken,
And took you for another.

Leon. [*Aside.*] In spite of all his guards, I'll see Palmyra;
Though meanly born, I have a kingly soul.

Amal. [*Aside.*] I stand upon a precipice, where fain
I would retire, but love still thrusts me on:
Now I grow bolder, and will speak to him.
— Sir, 'tis indeed to you that I would speak,
                    And if —

Leon. O, you are sent to scorn my fortunes?
Your sex and beauty are your privilege;
But should your brother —

Amal. [*Aside.*] Now he looks angry, and I dare not speak.—
I had some business with you, sir,
But 'tis not worth your knowledge.

Leon. Then 'twill be charity to let me mourn
My griefs alone, for I am much disordered.

Amal. 'Twill be more charity to mourn them with you:
Heaven knows I pity you.

Leon. Your pity, madam,
Is generous, but 'tis unavailable.

Amal. You know not till 'tis tried. Your sorrows are no secret;
You have lost a crown, and mistress.

Leon. Are not these enough?
Hang two such weights on any other soul,
And see if it can bear them.

Amal. More; you are banished, by my brother's means,
And ne'er must hope again to see your princess;
Except as prisoners view fair walks and streets,
And careless passengers going by their grates,
To make them feel the want of liberty.
But, worse than all, the king this morning has enjoined
His daughter to accept my brother's love.

Leon. Is this your pity? You aggravate my griefs,
And print them deeper, in new and heavier stamps.

Amal. 'Tis as physicians show the desperate ill,
To endear their art, by mitigating pains
They cannot wholly cure: When you despair
Of all you wish, some part of it, because
Unhoped for, may be grateful; and some other —

Leon. What other?

Amal. Some other may —
[*Aside.*]
My shame again
Has seized me, and I can go no farther.

Leon. These often failing sighs and interruptions
Make me imagine you have grief like mine:
Have you ne'er loved?

Amal.   I? Never! —
            [*Aside.*]
'Tis in vain: I must despair in silence.

Leon. You come, as I suspected then, to mock,
At least observe, my griefs: Take it not ill,
That I must leave you.
            [*Is going.*]

Amal. You must not go with these unjust opinions.
Command my life and fortunes: you are wise;
Think, and think well, what I can do to serve you.

Leon. I have but one thing in my thoughts and wishes:
If, by your means, I can obtain the sight
Of my adored Palmyra; or, what's harder,
One minute's time, to tell her, I die hers —
            [*She starts back.*]
I see I am not to expect it from you;
Nor could, indeed, with reason.

Amal. Name any other thing! Is Amalthea
So despicable, she can serve
Your wishes in this alone?

Leon. If I should ask of heaven, I have
            No other suit.

Amal. To show you, then, I can deny you nothing,
Though 'tis more hard to me than any other,
Yet I will do it for you.

Leon. Name quickly, name the means! Speak, my good angel!

Amal. Be not so much o'erjoyed; for, if you are,
I'll rather die than do't. This night the court
Will be in masquerade; you shall attend
On me; in that disguise. You may both see
And speak to her, if you dare venture it.

Leon. Yes; were a god her guardian, and
Bore in each hand thunder, I would venture.

Amal. Farewell, then; two hours hence I will expect you: — My
heart's so full, that I can stay no longer.

[*Exit.*]

Leon. Already it grows dusky: I'll prepare
With haste for my disguise. But who are these?

[*Enter* **Hermogenes** *and* **Eubulus**.]

Herm. 'Tis he; we need not fear to speak to him.

Eubu. Leonidas?

Leon.   Sure I have known that voice.

Herm. You have some reason, sir: 'tis Eubulus,
Who bred you with the princess; and, departing,
Bequeathed you to my care.

Leon. [*Kneeling.*] My foster-father! Let my knees express
My joys for your return!

Eubu.   Rise, sir; you must not kneel.

Leon. E'er since you left me,
I have been wandering in a maze of fate,
Led by false fires of a fantastic glory,
And the vain lustre of imagined crowns.
But, ah! Why would you leave me? Or how could you
Absent yourself so long?

Eubu. I'll give you a most just account of both:
And something more I have to tell you, which
I know must cause your wonder; but this place,
Though almost hid in darkness, is not safe.
Already I discern some coming towards us
        [*Torches appear.*]
With lights, who may discover me. Hermogenes,
Your lodgings are hard by, and much more private.

Herm. There you may freely speak.

Leon.   Let us make haste;
For some affairs, and of no small importance,
Call me another way.

                [*Exeunt.*]

SCENE II.

[*Enter* **Palamede** *and* **Rhodophil**, *with Vizor Masques in their Hands, and Torches before them.*]

Pala. We shall have noble sport to-night, Rhodophil; this masquerading is a most glorious invention.

Rhod. I believe it was invented first by some jealous lover, to discover the haunts of his jilting mistress; or, perhaps, by some distressed servant, to gain an opportunity with a jealous man's wife.

Pala. No, it must be the invention of a woman, it has so much of subtilty and love in it.

Rhod. I am sure 'tis extremely pleasant; for to go unknown, is the next degree to going invisible.

Pala. What with our antic habits and feigned voices — Do you know me? and — I know you — methinks we move and talk just like so many overgrown puppets.

Rhod. Masquerade is only vizor-mask improved; a heightening of the same fashion.

Pala. No, masquerade is vizor-mask in debauch, and I like it the better for't: for, with a vizor-mask, we fool ourselves into courtship, for the sake of an eye that glanced; or a hand that stole itself out of the glove sometimes, to give us a sample of the skin: But in masquerade there is nothing to be known, she's all terra incognita; and the bold discoverer leaps ashore, and takes his lot among the wild Indians and savages, without the vile consideration of safety to his person, or of beauty, or wholesomeness in his mistress.

[*Enter* **Beliza**.]

Rhod. Beliza, what make you here?

Beli. Sir, my lady sent me after you, to let you know, she finds herself a little indisposed; so that she cannot be at court, but is retired to rest in her own apartment, where she shall want the happiness of your dear embraces to night.

Rhod. A very fine phrase, Beliza, to let me know my wife desires to lie alone.

Pala. I doubt, Rhodophil, you take the pains sometimes to instruct your wife's woman in these elegancies.

Rhod. Tell my dear lady, that since I must be so unhappy as not to wait on her to-night, I will lament bitterly for her absence. 'Tis true I shall be at court, but I will take no divertisement there; and when I return to my solitary bed, if I am so forgetful of my passion as to sleep, I will dream of her; and betwixt sleep and waking, put out my foot towards her side, for midnight consolation; and, not finding her, I will sigh, and imagine myself a most desolate widower.

Beli. I shall do your commands, sir.

[*Exit.*]

Rhod. [*Aside.*] She's sick as aptly for my purpose, as if she had contrived it so. Well, if ever woman was a help-mate for man, my spouse is so; for within this hour I received a note from Melantha, that she would meet me this evening in masquerade, in boys' habit, to rejoice with me before she entered into fetters; for I find she loves me better than Palamede, only because he's to be her husband. There's something of antipathy in the word marriage to the nature of love: marriage is the mere ladle of affection, that cools it when 'tis never so fiercely boiling over.

Pala. Dear Rhodophil, I must needs beg your pardon; there is an occasion fallen out which I had forgot: I cannot be at court to-night.

Rhod. Dear Palamede, I am sorry we shall not have one course together at the herd; but I find your game lies single: Good fortune to you with your mistress.

[*Exit.*]

Pala. He has wished me good fortune with his wife; there's no sin in this then, there's fair leave given. Well, I must go visit the sick; I cannot resist the temptations of my charity. O what a difference will she find betwixt a dull resty husband and a quick vigorous lover! He sets out like a carrier's horse, plodding on, because he knows he must, with the bells of matrimony chiming so melancholy about his neck, in pain till he's at his journey's end; and, despairing to get thither, he is fain to fortify imagination with the thoughts of another woman: I take heat after heat, like a well-breathed courser, and — But hark, what noise is that? Swords!

[*Clashing of swords within.*]

Nay, then, have with you.

[*Exit* **Palamede**.]

[*Re-enter* **Palamede**, *with* **Rhodophil**; *and* **Doralice** *in man's habit.*]

Rhod. Friend, your relief was very timely, otherwise I had been oppressed.

Pala. What was the quarrel?

Rhod. What I did was in rescue of this youth.

Pala. What cause could he give them?

Dora. The cause was nothing but only the common cause of fighting in masquerades: They were drunk, as I was sober.

Rhod. Have they not hurt you?

Dora. No; but I am exceeding ill with the fright on't.

Pala. Let's lead him to some place, where he may refresh himself.

Rhod. Do you conduct him then.

Pala. [*Aside.*] How cross this happens to my design of going to Doralice! For I am confident she was sick on purpose that I should visit her. Hark you, Rhodophil, could not you take care of the stripling? I am partly engaged to-night.

Rhod. You know I have business; but come, youth, if it must be so.

Dora. [*to* **Rhodophil**.] No, good sir, do not give yourself that trouble; I shall be safer, and better pleased with your friend here.

Rhod. Farewell, then; once more I wish you a good adventure.

Pala. Damn this kindness! Now must I be troubled with this young rogue, and miss my opportunity with Doralice.

[*Exit* **Rhodophil** *alone;* **Palamede** *with* **Doralice**.]

SCENE III.

[*Enter* **Polydamus.**]

Poly. Argaleon counseled well to banish him:
He has, I know not what, of greatness
In his looks, and of high fate,
That almost awes me; but I fear my daughter,
Who hourly moves me for him; and I marked,
She sighed when I but named Argaleon to her.
But see, the maskers: Hence, my cares, this night!
At least take truce, and find me on my pillow.

> [*Enter* **Palmyra the Princess** *in masquerade, with* **Ladies**. *At the other end,* **Argaleon** *and* **Gentlemen** *in masquerade; then* **Leonidas** *leading* **Amalthea**. *The King sits. A Dance. After the Dance:*]

Amal. [*to* **Leonidas**.] That's the princess;
I saw the habit ere she put it on.

Leon. I know her by a thousand other signs;
She cannot hide so much divinity.
Disguised, and silent, yet some graceful motion
Breaks from her, and shines round her like a glory.
           [*Goes to* **Palmyra**.]

Amal. Thus she reveals herself, and knows it not;
Like love's dark lantern, I direct his steps,
And yet he sees not that, which gives him light.

Palm. I know you; but, alas! Leonidas,
Why should you tempt this danger on yourself?

Leon. Madam, you know me not, if you believe
I would not hazard greater for your sake.
But you, I fear, are changed.

Palm. No, I am still the same;
But there are many things became Palmyra,
Which ill become the princess.

Leon.   I ask nothing
Which honour will not give you leave to grant:

One hour's short audience, at my father's house,
You cannot sure refuse me.

Palm. Perhaps I should, did I consult strict virtue;
But something must be given to love and you.
When would you I should come?

Leon. This evening, with the speediest opportunity.
I have a secret to discover to you,
Which will surprise and please you.

Palm.   'Tis enough.
Go now; for we may be observed and known.
I trust your honour; give me not occasion
To blame myself, or you.

Leon. You never shall repent your good opinion.
              [*Kisses her hand, and Exit.*]

Arga. I cannot be deceived; that is the princess:
One of her maids betrayed the habit to me.
But who was he with whom she held discourse?
'Tis one she favours, for he kissed her hand.
Our shapes are like, our habits near the same;
She may mistake, and speak to me for him.
I am resolved; I'll satisfy my doubts,
Though to be more tormented.

SONG.

I.
Whilst Alexis lay pressed
In her arms he loved best,
With his hands round her neck, and his head on her breast,
He found the fierce pleasure too hasty to stay,
And his soul in the tempest just flying away.
II.
When Cælia saw this,
With a sigh and a kiss,
She cried, — O, my dear, I am robbed of my bliss!
'Tis unkind to your love, and unfaithfully done,
To leave me behind you, and die all alone.

III.
The youth, though in haste,
And breathing his last,
In pity died slowly, while she died more fast;
Till at length she cried, — Now, my dear, now let us go;
Now die, my Alexis, and I will die too!
IV.
Thus entranced they did lie,
Till Alexis did try
To recover new breath, that again he might die:
Then often they died; but the more they did so,
The nymph died more quick, and the shepherd more slow.

[*Another Dance. After it,* **Argaleon** *re-enters, and stands by the Princess.*]

Palm. [*To* **Argaleon**.] Leonidas, what means this quick return?

Arga. O heaven! 'Tis what I feared.

Palm. Is aught of moment happened since you went?

Arga. No, madam; but I understood not fully
Your last commands.

Palm. And yet you answered to them.
Retire; you are too indiscreet a lover:
I'll meet you where I promised.

[*Exit.*]

Arga. O my cursed fortune! What have I discovered!
But I will be revenged.
[*Whispers to the King.*]

Poly. But are you certain you are not deceived?

Arga. Upon my life.

Poly. Her honour is concerned.
Somewhat I'll do; but I am yet distracted,

And know not where to fix. I wished a child,
And heaven, in anger, granted my request.
So blind we are, our wishes are so vain,
That what we most desire, proves most our pain.

    [*Exeunt.*]

SCENE IV. — *An Eating-house.*

[*Bottles of Wine on the table.* **Palamede,** *and* **Doralice,** *in Man's Habit.*]

Dora. [*Aside.*] Now cannot I find in my heart to discover myself, though I long he should know me.

Pala. I tell thee, boy, now I have seen thee safe, I must be gone: I have no leisure to throw away on thy raw conversation; I am a person that understands better things, I.

Dora. Were I a woman, oh how you would admire me! Cry up every word I said, and screw your face into a submissive smile; as I have seen a dull gallant act wit, and counterfeit pleasantness, when he whispers to a great person in a play-house; smile, and look briskly, when the other answers, as if something of extraordinary had past betwixt them, when, heaven knows, there was nothing else but, — What o'clock does your lordship think it is? And my lord's repartee is, — It is almost park-time: or, at most, — Shall we out of the pit, and go behind the scenes for an act or two — And yet such fine things as these would be wit in a mistress's mouth.

Pala. Ay, boy; there dame Nature's in the case: He, who cannot find wit in a mistress, deserves to find nothing else, boy. But these are riddles to thee, child, and I have not leisure to instruct thee; I have affairs to dispatch, great affairs; I am a man of business.

Dora. Come, you shall not go: You have no affairs but what you may dispatch here, to my knowledge.

Pala. I find now, thou art a boy of more understanding than I thought thee; a very lewd wicked boy: O' my conscience, thou would'st debauch me, and hast some evil designs upon my person.

Dora. You are mistaken, sir; I would only have you show me a more lawful reason why you would leave me, than I can why you should not, and I'll not stay you; for I am not so young, but I understand the necessities of flesh and blood, and the pressing occasions of mankind, as well as you.

Pala. A very forward and understanding boy! Thou art in great danger of a page's wit, to be brisk at fourteen, and dull at twenty. But I'll give thee no further account; I must, and will go.

Dora. My life on it, your mistress is not at home.

Pala. This imp will make me very angry. I tell thee, young sir, she is at home, and at home for me; and, which is more, she is a-bed for me, and sick for me.

Dora. For you only?

Pala. Aye, for me only.

Dora. But how do you know she's sick a-bed?

Pala. She sent her husband word so.

Dora. And are you such a novice in love, to believe a wife's message to her husband?

Pala. Why, what the devil should be her meaning else?

Dora. It may be, to go in masquerade, as well as you; to observe your haunts, and keep you company without your knowledge.

Pala. Nay, I'll trust her for that: She loves me too well, to disguise herself from me.

Dora. If I were she, I would disguise on purpose to try your wit; and come to my servant like a riddle, — Read me, and take me.

Pala. I could know her in any shape: My good genius would prompt me to find out a handsome woman: There's something that would attract me to her without my knowledge.

Dora. Then you make a loadstone of your mistress?

Pala. Yes, and I carry steel about me, which has been so often touched that it never fails to point to the north pole.

Dora. Yet still my mind gives me, that you have met her disguised to-night, and have not known her.

Pala. This is the most pragmatical conceited little fellow, he will needs understand my business better than myself. I tell thee, once more, thou dost not know my mistress.

Dora. And I tell you once more, that I know her better than you do.

Pala. The boy's resolved to have the last word. I find I must go without reply.

[*Exit.*]

Dora. Ah mischief, I have lost him with my fooling. Palamede, Palamede!

[*He returns. She plucks off her peruke, and puts it on again when he knows her.*]

Pala. O heavens! Is it you, madam?

Dora. Now, where was your good genius, that would prompt you to find me out?

Pala. Why, you see I was not deceived; you yourself were my good genius.

Dora. But where was the steel, that knew the loadstone? Ha?

Pala. The truth is, madam, the steel has lost its virtue: and, therefore, if you please, we'll new touch it.

[*Enter* **Rhodophil**; *and* **Melantha** *in Boys habit.* **Rhodophil** *sees* **Palamede** *kissing* **Doralice**'s *hand.*]

Rhod. Palamede again! Am I fallen into your quarters? What? Engaging with a boy? Is all honourable?

Pala. O, very honourable on my side. I was just chastising this young villain; he was running away, without paying his share of the reckoning.

Rhod. Then I find I was deceived in him.

Pala. Yes, you are deceived in him: 'tis the archest rogue, if you did but know him.

Mela. Good Rhodophil, let us get off *a-la derobbée*, for fear I should be discovered.

Rhod. There's no retiring now; I warrant you for discovery. Now have I the oddest thought, to entertain you before your servant's face, and he never the wiser; it will be the prettiest juggling trick, to cheat him when he looks upon us.

Mela. This is the strangest caprice in you.

Pala. [*to* **Doralice**.] This Rhodophil's the unluckiest fellow to me! This is now the second time he has barred the dice when we were just ready to have nicked him; but if ever I get the box again —

Dora. Do you think he will not know me? Am I like myself?

Pala. No more than a picture in the hangings.

Dora. Nay, then he can never discover me, now the wrong side of the arras is turned towards him.

Pala. At least, it will be some pleasure to me, to enjoy what freedom I can while he looks on; I will storm the out-works of matrimony even before his face.

Rhod. What wine have you there, Palamede?

Pala. Old Chios, or the rogue's damn'd that drew it.

Rhod. Come, — to the most constant of mistresses! That, I believe, is yours, Palamede.

Dora. Pray spare your seconds; for my part I am but a weak brother.

Pala. Now, — to the truest of turtles! That is your wife, Rhodophil, that lies sick at home, in the bed of honour.

Rhod. Now let us have one common health, and so have done.

Dora. Then, for once, I'll begin it. Here's to him that has the fairest lady of Sicily in masquerade to night.

Pala. This is such an obliging health, I'll kiss thee, dear rogue, for thy invention.

[*Kisses her.*]

Rhod. He, who has this lady, is a happy man, without dispute.
[*Aside.*]
I'm most concerned in this, I am sure.

Pala. Was it not well found out, Rhodophil?

Mela. Ay, this was *bien trouvée* indeed.

Dora. [*to* **Melantha**.] I suppose I shall do you a kindness, to enquire if you have not been in France, sir?

Mela. To do you service, sir.

Dora. [*Saluting her.*] O, monsieur, *votre valet bien humble.*

Mela. [*Returning the salute.*] *Votre esclave, monsieur, de tout mon cœur.*

Dora. I suppose, sweet sir, you are the hope and joy of some thriving citizen, who has pinched him self at home, to breed you abroad, where you have learned your exercises, as it appears, most awkwardly, and are returned, with the addition of a new-laced bosom and a clap, to your good old father, who looks at you with his mouth, while you spout French with your *man monsieur*.

Pala. Let me kiss thee again for that, dear rogue.

Mela. And you, I imagine, are my young master, whom your mother durst not trust upon salt-water, but left you to be your own tutor at fourteen, to be very brisk and *entreprenant*, to *endeavour* to be debauched ere you have learned the knack of it, to value yourself upon a clap before you can get it, and to make it the height of your ambition to get a player for your mistress.

Rhod. [*embracing* **Melantha**.] O dear young bully thou hast tickled him with a repartee, i'faith.

Mela. You are one of those that applaud our country plays, where drums, and trumpets, and blood, and wounds, are wit.

Rhod. Again, my boy? Let me kiss thee most abundantly.

Dora. You are an admirer of the dull French poetry, which is so thin, that it is the very leaf-gold of wit, the very wafers and whip'd cream of sense, for which a man opens his mouth, and gapes, to swallow nothing: And to be an admirer of such profound dulness, one must be endowed with a great perfection of impudence and ignorance.

Pala. Let me embrace thee most vehemently.

Mela. [*Advancing*.] I'll sacrifice my life for French poetry.

Dora. I'll die upon the spot for our country wit.

Rhod. [*to* **Melantha**.] Hold, hold, young Mars! Palamede, draw back your hero.

Pala. 'Tis time; I shall be drawn in for a second else at the wrong weapon.

Mela. O that I were a man, for thy sake!

Dora. You'll be a man as soon as I shall.

[*Enter a* **Messenger** *to* **Rhodophil**.]

Mess. Sir, the king has instant business with you;
I saw the guard drawn up by your lieutenant,
Before the palace-gate, ready to march.

Rhod. 'Tis somewhat sudden; say that I am coming.
[*Exit* **Messenger**.]
Now, Palamede, what think you of this sport?
This is some sudden tumult; will you along?

Pala. Yes, yes, I will go; but the devil take me if ever I was less in humour. Why the pox could they not have stayed their tumult till tomorrow? Then I had done my business, and been ready for them. Truth is, I had a little transitory crime to have committed first; and I am the worst man in the world at repenting, till a sin be thoroughly done: But what shall we do with the two boys?

Rhod. Let them take a lodging in the house, 'till the business be over.

Dora. What, lie with a boy? For my part, I own it, I cannot endure to lie with a boy.

Pala. The more's my sorrow, I cannot accommodate you with a better bed-fellow.

Mela. Let me die, if I enter into a pair of sheets with him that hates the French.

Dora. Pish, take no care for us, but leave us in the streets; I warrant you, as late as it is, I'll find my lodging as well as any drunken bully of them all.

Rhod. I'll light in mere revenge, and wreak my passion, —
   [*Aside.*]
On all that spoil this hopeful assignation.

Pala. I'm sure we light in a good quarrel:
Rogues may pretend religion, and the laws;
But a kind mistress is the good old cause.

   [*Exuent.*]

SCENE V.

[*Enter* **Palmyra, Eubulus,** *and* **Hermogenes.**]

Palm. You tell me wonders; that Leonidas
Is prince Theagenes, the late king's son.

Eubu. It seems as strange to him, as now to you,
Before I had convinced him; but, besides
His great resemblance to the king his father,
The queen his mother lives, secured by me
In a religious house, to whom, each year,
I brought the news of his increasing virtues.
My last long absence from you both was caused
By wounds, which in my journey I received,
When set upon by thieves; I lost those jewels
And letters, which your dying mother left.

Herm. The same he means, which, since, brought to the king,
Made him first know he had a child alive:
'Twas then my care of prince Leonidas,
Caused me to say he was the usurper's son;
Till after, forced by your apparent danger,
I made the true discovery of your birth,
And once more hid my prince's.

[*Enter* **Leonidas.**]

Leon. Hermogenes, and Eubulus, retire;
Those of our party, whom I left without,
Expect your aid and counsel.

[*Exeunt* **Hermogenes** *and* **Eubulus.**]

Palm. I should, Leonidas, congratulate
This happy change of your exalted fate;
But, as my joy, so you my wonder move.
Your looks have more of business than of love;
And your last words some great design did shew.

Leon. I frame not any to be hid from you;
You, in my love, all my designs may see.
But what have love and you designed for me?
Fortune, once more, has set the balance right;

First, equalled us in lowness; then, in height.
Both of us have so long, like gamesters, thrown,
Till fate comes round, and gives to each his own.
As fate is equal, so may love appear:
Tell me, at least, what I must hope, or fear.

Palm. After so many proofs, how can you call
My love in doubt? Fear nothing, and hope all.
Think what a prince, with honour, may receive,
Or I may give, without a parent's leave.

Leon. You give, and then restrain the grace you show;
As ostentatious priests, when souls they woo,
Promise their heaven to all, but grant to few.
But do for me, what I have dared for you:
I did no argument from duty bring;
Duty's a name, and love's a real thing.

Palm. Man's love may, like wild torrents, overflow;
Woman's as deep, but in its banks must go.
My love is mine, and that I can impart;
But cannot give my person, with my heart.

Leon. Your love is then no gift:
For, when the person it does not convey,
'Tis to give gold, and not to give the key.

Palm. Then ask my father.

Leon. He detains my throne;
Who holds back mine, will hardly give his own.

Palm. What then remains?

Leon. That I must have recourse
To arms, and take my love and crown, by force.
Hermogenes is forming the design;
And with him all the brave and loyal join.

Palm. And is it thus you court Palmyra's bed?
Can she the murderer of her parent wed?
Desist from force: So much you well may give
To love, and me, to let my father live.

Leon. Each act of mine my love to you has shown;
But you who tax my want of it, have none.
You bid me part with you, and let him live;
But they should nothing ask, who nothing give.

Palm. I give what virtue, and what duty can,
In vowing ne'er to wed another man.

Leon. You will be forced to be Argaleon's wife.

Palm. I'll keep my promise, though I lose my life.

Leon. Then you lose love, for which we both contend;
For life is but the means, but love's the end.

Palm. Our souls shall love hereafter.

Leon.   I much fear,
That soul, which could deny the body here
To taste of love, would be a niggard there.

Palm. Then 'tis past hope: our cruel fate, I see,
Will make a sad divorce 'twixt you and me.
For, if you force employ, by heav'n I swear,
And all blessed beings, —

Leon.   Your rash oath forbear.

Palm. I never —

Leon. Hold once more. But yet, as he,
Who 'scapes a dangerous leap, looks back to see;
So I desire, now I am past my fear,
To know what was that oath you meant to swear.

Palm. I meant, that if you hazarded your life,
Or sought my father's, ne'er to be your wife.

Leon. See now, Palmyra, how unkind you prove!
Could you, with so much ease, forswear my love?

Palm. You force me with your ruinous design.

Leon. Your father's life is more your care, than mine.

Palm. You wrong me: 'Tis not, though it ought to be;
You are my care, heaven knows, as well as he.

Leon. If now the execution I delay,
My honour, and my subjects, I betray.
All is prepared for the just enterprise;
And the whole city will tomorrow rise.
The leaders of the party are within,
And Eubulus has sworn that he will bring,
To head their arms, the person of their king.

Palm. In telling this, you may be guilty too;
I therefore must discover what I know:
What honour bids you do, nature bids me prevent;
But kill me first, and then pursue your black intent.

Leon. Palmyra, no; you shall not heed to die;
Yet I'll not trust so strict a piety.
Within there!
        [*Enter* **Eubulus**.]
        Eubulus, a guard prepare;
Here, I commit this prisoner to your care.
        [*Kisses* **Palmyra**'s *hand, then gives it to* **Eubulus**.]

Palm. Leonidas, I never thought these bands
Could e'er be given me by a lover's hands.

Leon. Palmyra, thus your judge himself arraigns;
        [*Kneeling*.]
He, who imposed these bands, still wears your chains:
When you to love or duty false must be,
Or to your father guilty, or to me,
These chains, alone, remain to set you free.

        [*Noise of swords clashing*.]

Poly. [*Within*.] Secure these, first: then search the inner room.

Leon. From whence do these tumultuous clamours come?

        [*Enter* **Hermogenes**, *hastily*.]

Herm. We are betrayed; and there remains alone
This comfort, that your person is not known.

[*Enter* **the King, Argaleon, Rhodophil, Palamede, Guards**; *some like* **Citizens**, *as prisoners.*]

Poly. What mean these midnight consultations here,
Where I like an unsummoned guest appear?

Leon. Sir —

Arga. There needs no excuse; 'tis understood;
You were all watching for your prince's good.

Poly. My reverend city friends, you are well met!
On what great work were your grave wisdoms set?
Which of my actions were you scanning here?
What French invasion have you found to fear?

Leon. They are my friends; and come, sir, with intent,
To take their leaves, before my banishment.

Poly. Your exile in both sexes friends can find:
          [*Seeing* **Palmyra**.]
I see the ladies, like the men, are kind.

Palm. [*Kneeling.*] Alas, I came but —

Poly.   Add not to your crime
A lie: I'll hear you speak some other time.
How? Eubulus! Nor time, nor thy disguise,
Can keep thee undiscovered from my eyes.
A guard there! Seize them all.

Rhod. Yield, sir; what use of valour can be shown?

Pala. One, and unarmed, against a multitude!

Leon. Oh for a sword!
    [*He reaches at one of the* **Guards**' *halberds, and is seized behind.*]
                I wonnot lose my breath
In fruitless prayers; but beg a speedy death.

Palm. O spare Leonidas, and punish me!

Poly. Mean girl, thou want'st an advocate for thee.
Now the mysterious knot will be untied;
Whether the young king lives, or where he died:
Tomorrow's dawn shall the dark riddle clear,
Crown all my joys, and dissipate my fear.

[*Exeunt.*]

ACT V. SCENE I.

[**Palamede, Strato. Palamede** with a letter in his hand.]

Pala. This evening, sayest thou? Will they both be here?

Stra. Yes, sir, both my old master, and your mistress's father. The old gentlemen ride hard this journey; they say, it shall be the last time they will see the town; and both of them are so pleased with this marriage, which they have concluded for you, that I am afraid they will live some years longer to trouble you, with the joy of it.

Pala. But this is such an unreasonable thing, to impose upon me to be married tomorrow; 'tis hurrying a man to execution, without giving him time to say his prayers.

Stra. Yet, if I might advise you, sir, you should not delay it; for your younger brother comes up with them, and is got already into their favours. He has gained much upon my old master, by finding fault with innkeepers' bills, and by starving us, and our horses, to show his frugality; and he is very well with your mistress's father, by giving him recipes for the spleen, gout and scurvy, and other infirmities of old age.

Pala. I'll rout him, and his country education: Pox on him, I remember him before I traveled, he had nothing in him but mere jockey; used to talk loud, and make matches, and was all for the crack of the field: Sense and wit were as much banished from his discourse, as they are when the court goes out of town to a horse race. Go now and provide your master's lodgings.

Stra. I go, sir.

[*Exit.*]

Pala. It vexes me to the heart, to leave all my designs with Doralice unfinished; to have flown her so often to a mark, and still to be bobbed at retrieve: If I had once enjoyed her, though I could not have satisfied my stomach with the feast, at least I should have relished my mouth a little; but now —

[*Enter* **Philotis.**]

Phil. Oh, sir, you are happily met; I was coming to find you.

Pala. From your lady. I hope.

Phil. Partly from her; but more especially from myself: She has just now received a letter from her father, with an absolute command to dispose herself to marry you tomorrow.

Pala. And she takes it to the death?

Phil. Quite contrary: The letter could never have come in a more lucky minute; for it found her in an ill-humour with a rival of yours, that shall be nameless, about the pronunciation of a French word.

Pala. Count Rhodophil? Never disguise it, I know the amour: But I hope you took the occasion to strike in for me?

Phil. It was my good fortune to do you some small service in it; for your sake I discommended him all over, — clothes, person, humour, behaviour, every thing; and, to sum up all, told her, it was impossible to find a married man that was otherwise; for they were all so mortified at home with their wives' ill humours, that they could never recover themselves to be company abroad.

Pala. Most divinely urged!

Phil. Then I took occasion to commend your good qualities; as the sweetness of your humour, the comeliness of your person, your good mein, your valour; but, above all, your liberality.

Pala. I vow to God I had like to have forgot that good quality in myself, if thou hadst not remembered me of it: Here are five pieces for thee.

Phil. Lord, you have the softest hand, sir, it would do a woman good to touch it: Count Rhodophil's is not half so soft; for I remember I felt it once, when he gave me ten pieces for my new-years-gift.

Pala. O, I understand you, madam; you shall find my hand as soft again as Count Rhodophil's: There are twenty pieces for you. The former was but a retaining fee; now I hope you'll plead for me.

Phil. Your own merits speak enough. Be sure only to ply her with French words, and I'll warrant you'll do your business. Here are a list of her phrases for this day: Use them to her upon all occasions and foil her at her own weapon; for she's like one of the old Amazons, she'll never marry, except it be the man who has first conquered her.

Pala. I'll be sure to follow your advice: But you'll forget to further my design.

Phil. What, do you think I'll be ungrateful? — But however, if you distrust my memory, put some token on my finger to remember it by: That diamond there would do admirably.

Pala. There 'tis; and I ask your pardon heartily for calling your memory into question: I assure you I'll trust it another time, without putting you to the trouble of another token.

[*Enter* **Palmyra** *and* **Artemis**.]

Arte. Madam, this way the prisoners are to pass; Here you may see Leonidas.

Palm. Then here I'll stay, and follow him to death.

[*Enter* **Melantha**, *hastily*.]

Mela. O, here's her highness! Now is my time to introduce myself, and to make my court to her, in my new French phrases. Stay, let me read my catalogue — *Suite, figure, chagrin, naiveté,* and *let me die,* for the parenthesis of all.

Pala. [*Aside.*] Do, persecute her; and I'll persecute thee as fast in thy own dialect.

Mela. Madam, the princess! Let me die, but this is a most horrid spectacle, to see a person, who makes so grand a *figure* in the court, without the *suite* of a princess, and entertaining your *chagrin* all alone —
    [*Aside.*]
Naiveté should have been there, but the disobedient word would not come in.

Palm. What is she, Artemis?

Arte. An impertinent lady, madam; very ambitious of being known to your highness.

Pala. [*To* **Melantha**.] Let me die, madam, if I have not waited you here these two long hours, without so much as the *suite* of a single servant to attend me; entertaining myself with my own *chagrin* till I had the honour of seeing your ladyship, who are a person that makes so considerable a *figure* in the court.

Mela. Truce with your *douceurs*, good servant; you see I am addressing to the princess; pray do not embarrass me — Embarrass me! What a delicious French word do you make me lose upon you too!
[*To the* **Princess**.]
Your highness, madam, will please to pardon the *beveue* which I made, in not sooner finding you out to be a princess: But let me die if this *eclaircissement*, which is made this day of your quality, does not ravish me; and give me leave to tell you —

Pala. But first give me leave to tell you, madam, that I have so great a *tendre* for your person, and such a *penchant* to do you service, that —

Mela. What, must I still be troubled with your *sottises*? (There's another word lost, that I meant for the princess, with a mischief to you!) But your highness, madam —

Pala. But your ladyship, madam —

[*Enter* **Leonidas**, *guarded and led over the stage.*]

Mela. Out upon him, how he looks, madam! Now he's found no prince, he is the strangest *figure* of a man; how could I make that *coup d'etourdi* to think him one?

Palm. Away, impertinent! My dear Leonidas!

Leon. My dear Palmyra!

Palm. Death shall never part us; my destiny is yours.

[*He is led off, she follows.*]

Mela. Impertinent! Oh I am the most unfortunate person this day breathing: That the princess should thus *rompre en visiere*, without occasion. Let me die, but I'll follow her to death, till I make my peace.

Pala. [*Holding her.*] And let me die, but I'll follow you to the *infernals*, till you pity me.

Mela. [*Turning towards him angrily.*] Ay, 'tis long of you that this *malheur* is fallen upon me; your impertinence has put me out of the good graces of the princess, and all that, which has ruined me, and all that, and, therefore, let me die, but I'll be revenged, and all that.

Pala. Façon, façon, you must and shall love me, and all that; for my old man is coming up, and all that; and I am *desesperé au dernier,* and will not be disinherited, and all that.

Mela. How durst you interrupt me so mal apropos, when you knew I was addressing to the princess?

Pala. But why would you address yourself so much a *contretemps* then?

Mela. Ah, *mal peste!*

Pala. Ah, *j'enrage!*

Phil. Radoucissez vous, de grace, madame; vous étes bien en colere pour peu de chose. Vous n'entendez pas la raillerie gallante.

Mela. Ad autres, ad autres: He mocks himself of me, he abuses me: Ah me unfortunate!
        [*Cries.*]

Phil. You mistake him, madam, he does but accommodate his phrase to your refined language. *Ah qu'il est un cavalier accompli!*
        [*To him.*]
Pursue your point, sir —

Pala. [*Singing.*] *Ah qu'il fait beau dans ces boccages; Ah que le ciet donne un beau jour!* — There I was with you, with a *minuét.*

Mela. Let me die now, but this singing is fine, and extremely French in him:
 [*Laughs.*]
But then, that he should use my own words, as it were in contempt of me —
 [*Crying.*]
— I cannot bear it!

Pala. [*Singing.*] Ces beaux sejours, ces doux ramages —

Mela. [*Singing after him.*] Ces beaux sejours, ces doux ramages. Ces beaux sejours nous invitent á l'amour!
 [*Laughing.*]
Let me die, but he sings *en cavalier*, and so humours the cadence!

Pala. [*Singing again.*] Foy, ma Clymene, voy sous ce chene. S'entrebaiser ces oiseaux amoreux! Let me die now, but that was fine. Ah, now, for three or four brisk Frenchmen, to be put into masking habits, and to sing it on a theatre, how witty it would be! And then to dance helter skelter to a *chanson a boire: Toute la terre, toute la terre est a moi!* What's matter though it were made and sung two or three years ago in *cabarets*, how it would attract the admiration, especially of every one that's an *eveillé*!

Mela. Well; I begin to have a *tendre* for you; but yet, upon condition, that — when we are married, you —
 [**Palamede** *sings, while she speaks.*]

Phil. You must drown her voice: If she makes her French conditions, you are a slave for ever.

Mela. First, you will engage — that —

Pala. [*Louder.*] Fa, la, la, la, &c.

Mela. Will you hear the conditions?

Pala. No; I will hear no conditions; I am resolved to win you *en François*: To be very airy, with abundance of noise, and no sense: Fa la, la, la, &c.

Mela. Hold, hold: I am vanquished with your *gayeté d'esprit*. I am yours, and will be yours, *sans nulle reserve, ni condition*: And let me die, if I do not think myself the happiest nymph in Sicily — My dear French dear, stay but a *minuite*, till I *raccommode* myself with the princess; and then I am yours, *jusqu' a la mort. Allons donc.*

[*Exeunt* **Melantha** *and* **Philotis**.]

Pala. [*Solus, fanning himself with his hat.*] I never thought before that wooing was so laborious an exercise; if she were worth a million, I have deserved her; and now, methinks too, with taking all this pains for her, I begin to like her. 'Tis so; I have known many, who never cared for hare nor partridge, but those they caught themselves would eat heartily: The pains, and the story a man tells of the taking them, makes the meat go down more pleasantly. Besides, last night I had a sweet dream of her, and, gad, she I have once dreamed of, I am stark mad till I enjoy her, let her be never so ugly.

[*Enter* **Doralice**.]

Dora. Who's that you are so mad to enjoy, Palamede?

Pala. You may easily imagine that, sweet Doralice.

Dora. More easily than you think I can: I met just now with a certain man, who came to you with letters from a certain old gentleman, ycleped your father; whereby I am given to understand, that tomorrow you are to take an oath in the church to be grave henceforward, to go ill-dressed and slovenly, to get heirs for your estate, and to dandle them for your diversion; and, in short, that love and courtship are to be no more.

Pala. Now have I so much shame to be thus apprehended in the manner, that I can neither speak nor look upon you; I have abundance of grace in me, that I find: But if you have any spark of true friendship in you, retire with me a little into the next room, that hath a couch or bed in it, and bestow your charity upon a dying man! A little comfort from a mistress, before a man is going to give himself in marriage, is as good as a lusty dose of strong-water to a dying malefactor: it takes away the sense of hell and hanging from him.

Dora. No, good Palamede, I must not be so injurious to your bride: 'Tis ill drawing from the bank today, when all your ready money is payable tomorrow.

Pala. A wife is only to have the ripe fruit, that falls of itself; but a wise man will always preserve a shaking for a mistress.

Dora. But a wife for the first quarter is a mistress.

Pala. But when the second comes —

Dora. When it does come, you are so given to variety, that you would make a wife of me in another quarter.

Pala. No, never, except I were married to you: married people can never oblige one another; for all they do is duty, and consequently there can be no thanks: But love is more frank and generous than he is honest; he's a liberal giver, but a cursed pay-master.

Dora. I declare I will have no gallant; but, if I would, he should never be a married man; a married man is but a mistress's half-servant, as a clergyman is but the king's half-subject: For a man to come to me that smells of the wife! 'Slife, I would as soon wear her old gown after her, as her husband.

Pala. Yet 'tis a kind of fashion to wear a princess's cast shoes; you see the country ladies buy them, to be fine in them.

Dora. Yes, a princess's shoes may be worn after her, because they keep their fashion, by being so very little used; but generally a married man is the creature of the world the most out of fashion: his behaviour is dumpish; his discourse, his wife and family; his habit so much neglected, it looks as if that were married too; his hat is married, his peruke is married, his breeches are married, and, if we could look within his breeches, we should find him married there too.

Pala. Am I then to be discarded forever? Pray do but mark how that word sounds: forever! It has a very damn'd sound, Doralice.

Dora. Ay, forever! It sounds as hellishly to me, as it can do to you, but there's no help for it.

Pala. Yet, if we had but once enjoyed one another! — but then once only, is worse than not at all: It leaves a man with such a lingering after it.

Dora. For aught I know, 'tis better that we have not; we might upon trial have liked each other less, as many a man and woman, that have loved as desperately as we, and yet, when they came to possession, have sighed and cried to themselves, 'Is this all?'

Pala. That is only, if the servant were not found a man of this world; but if, upon trial, we had not liked each other, we had certainly left loving; and faith, that's the greater happiness of the two.

Dora. 'Tis better as 'tis; we have drawn off already as much of our love as would run clear; after possessing, the rest is but jealousies, and disquiets, and quarrelling, and piecing.

Pala. Nay, after one great quarrel, there's never any sound piecing; the love is apt to break in the same place again.

Dora. I declare I would never renew a love; that's like him, who trims an old coach for ten years together; he might buy a new one better cheap.

Pala. Well, madam, I am convinced, that 'tis best for us not to have enjoyed; but, gad, the strongest reason is, because I can't help it.

Dora. The only way to keep us new to one another is never to enjoy, as they keep grapes, by hanging them upon a line; they must touch nothing, if you would preserve them fresh.

Pala. But then they wither, and grow dry in the very keeping; however, I shall have a warmth for you, and an eagerness, every time I see you; and, if I chance to out-live Melantha —

Dora. And if I chance to out-live Rhodophil —

Pala. Well, I'll cherish my body as much as I can, upon that hope. 'Tis true, I would not directly murder the wife of my bosom; but, to kill her civilly, by the way of kindness, I'll put as fair as another man: I'll begin tomorrow night, and be very wrathful with her; that's resolved on.

Dora. Well, Palamede, here's my hand, I'll venture to be your second wife, for all your threatenings.

Pala. In the meantime I'll watch you hourly, as I would the ripeness of a melon; and I hope you'll give me leave now and then to look on you, and to see if you are not ready to be cut yet.

Dora. No, no, that must not be, Palamede, for fear the gardener should come and catch you taking up the glass.

[*Enter* **Rhodophil**.]

Rhod. [*Aside.*] Billing so sweetly! Now I am confirmed in my suspicions; I must put an end to this ere it go farther —
[*To* **Doralice**.]
Cry you mercy, spouse, I fear I have interrupted your recreations.

Dora. What recreations?

Rhod. Nay, no excuses, good spouse; I saw fair hand conveyed to lip, and pressed, as though you had been squeezing soft wax together for an indenture. Palamede, you and I must clear this reckoning: why would you have seduced my wife?

Pala. Why would you have debauched my mistress?

Rhod. What do you think of that civil couple, that played at a game, called Hide and Seek, last evening in the grotto?

Pala. What do you think of that innocent pair, who made it their pretence to seek for others, but came, indeed, to hide themselves there?

Rhod. All things considered, I begin vehemently to suspect, that the young gentleman I found in your company last night, was a certain youth of my acquaintance.

Pala. And I have an odd imagination, that you could never have suspected my small gallant, if your little villainous Frenchman had not been a false brother.

Rhod. Further arguments are needless; draw off; I shall speak to you now by the way of Bilbo.
[*Claps his hand to his sword.*]

Pala. And I shall answer you by the way of Dangerfield.
[*Claps his hand on his.*]

Dora. Hold, hold; are not you two a couple of mad fighting fools, to cut one another's throats for nothing?

Pala. How for nothing? He courts the woman I must marry.

Rhod. And he courts you, whom I have married.

Dora. But you can neither of you be jealous of what you love not.

Rhod. Faith, I am jealous, and this makes me partly suspect that I love you better than I thought.

Dora. Pish! A mere jealousy of honour.

Rhod. Gad, I am afraid there's something else in't; for Palamede has wit, and, if he loves you, there's something more in ye than I have found: Some rich mine, for aught I know, that I have not yet discovered.

Pala. 'Slife, what's this? Here's an argument for me to love Melantha; for he has loved her, and he has wit too, and, for aught I know, there may be a mine; but, if there be, I am resolved I'll dig for it.

Dora. [*To* **Rhodophil.**] Then I have found my account in raising your jealousy. O! 'Tis the most delicate sharp sauce to a cloyed stomach; it will give you a new edge, Rhodophil.

Rhod. And a new point too, Doralice, if I could be sure thou art honest.

Dora. If you are wise, believe me for your own sake: Love and religion have but one thing to trust to; that's a good sound faith. Consider, if I have played false, you can never find it out by any experiment you can make upon me.

Rhod. No? Why, suppose I had a delicate screwed gun; if I left her clean, and found her foul, I should discover, to my cost, she had been shot in.

Dora. But if you left her clean, and found her only rusty, you would discover, to your shame, she was only so for want of shooting.

Pala. Rhodophil, you know me too well to imagine I speak for fear; and therefore, in consideration of our past friendship, I will tell you, and bind it by all things holy, that Doralice is innocent.

Rhod. Friend, I will believe you, and vow the same for your Melantha; but the devil on't is, how shall we keep them so?

Pala. What dost think of a blessed community betwixt us four, for the solace of the women, and relief of the men? Methinks it would be a pleasant kind of life: Wife and husband for the standing dish, and mistress and gallant for the dessert.

Rhod. But suppose the wife and mistress should both long for the standing dish, how should they be satisfied together?

Pala. In such a case they must draw lots; and yet that would not do neither, for they would both be wishing for the longest cut.

Rhod. Then I think, Palamede, we had as good make a firm league, not to invade each other's propriety.

Pala. Content, say I. From henceforth let all acts of hostility cease betwixt us; and that, in the usual form of treaties, as well by sea as land, and in all fresh waters.

Dora. I will add but one proviso, that whoever breaks the league, either by war abroad, or neglect at home, both the women shall revenge themselves by the help of the other party.

Rhod. That's but reasonable. Come away, Doralice; I have a great temptation to be sealing articles in private.

Pala. Hast thou so?
  [*Claps him on the shoulder.*]
"Fall on, Macduff, And cursed be he that first cries, 'Hold, enough.'"

[*Enter* **Polydamas, Palmyra, Artemis, Argaleon**: *After them* **Eubulus** *and* **Hermogenes**, *guarded.*]

Palm. Sir, on my knees I beg you —

Poly.   Away, I'll hear no more.

Palm. For my dead mother's sake; you say you loved her,
And tell me I resemble her. Thus she
Had begged.

Poly.   And thus I had denied her.

Palm. You must be merciful.

Arga.   You must be constant.

Poly. Go, bear them to the torture; you have boasted
You have a king to head you; I would know
To whom I must resign.

Eubu.   This is our recompence
 For serving thy dead queen.

Herm.   And education
Of thy daughter.

Arga. You are too modest, in not naming all
His obligations to you: Why did you
Omit his son, the prince Leonidas?

Poly.   That imposture
I had forgot; their tortures shall be doubled.

Herm. You please me; I shall die the sooner.

Eubu. [*As they are going off.*] No; could I live an age, and still be racked,
I still would keep the secret.

[*Enter* **Leonidas**, *guarded.*]

Leon. Oh, whither do you hurry innocence!
If you have any justice, spare their lives;
Or, if I cannot make you just, at least
I'll teach you to more purpose to be cruel.

Palm. Alas, what does he seek!

Leon. Make me the object of your hate and vengeance:

Are these decrepid bodies, worn to ruin,
Just ready of themselves to fall asunder.
And to let drop the soul —
Are these fit subjects for a rack and tortures?
Where would you fasten any hold upon them?
Place pains on me, — united fix them here —
I have both youth, and strength, and soul to bear them;
And, if they merit death, then I much more,
Since 'tis for me they suffer.

Herm. Heaven forbid
We should redeem our pains, or worthless lives,
By our exposing yours.

Eubu. Away with us.
Farewell, sir: I only suffer in my fears for you.

Arga. [*Aside.*] So much concerned for him! Then my
Suspicion's true.
[*Whispers to the* **King**.]

Palm. Hear yet my last request for poor Leonidas,
Or take my life with his.

Arga. [*To the* **King**.] Rest satisfied, Leonidas is he.

Poly. I am amazed: What must be done?

Arga. Command his execution instantly:
Give him not leisure to discover it;
He may corrupt the soldiers.

Poly. Hence with that traitor, bear him to his death:
Haste there, and see my will performed.

Leon. Nay, then, I'll die like him the gods have made me.
Hold, gentlemen, I am —

[**Argaleon** *stops his mouth.*]

Arga. Thou art a traitor; 'tis not fit to hear thee.

Leon. [*Getting loose a little.*] I say, I am the —

Arga. [*Again stopping his mouth.*] So; gag him, and lead him off.

[**Leonidas, Hermogenes, Eubulus,** *led off;*
Polydamas *and* **Argaleon** *follow.*]

Palm. Duty and love, by turns, possess my soul
And struggle for a fatal victory.
I will discover he's the king: — Ah, no!
That will perhaps save him;
But then I'm guilty of a father's ruin.
What shall I do, or not do? Either way
I must destroy a parent, or a lover.
Break heart; for that's the least of ills to me,
        And death the only cure.
      [*Swoons.*]

Arte. Help, help the princess!

Rhod. Bear her gently hence, where she may
        Have more succour.

[*She is borne off;* **Artemis** *follows her.*]
[*Shouts within, and clashing of swords.*]

Pala. What noise is that?

[*Enter* **Amalthea,** *running.*]

Amal. Oh, gentlemen, if you have loyalty,
Or courage, show it now! Leonidas,
Broke on the sudden from his guards, and snatching
A sword from one, his back against the scaffold,
Bravely defends himself, and owns aloud
He is our long-lost king; found for this moment,
But, if your valour helps not, lost for ever.
Two of his guards, moved by the sense of virtue,
Are turned for him, and there they stand at bay
Against an host of foes.

Rhod.   Madam, no more;
We lose time; my command, or my example,
May move the soldiers to the better cause.
      [*To* **Palamede.**]
You'll second me?

Pala. Or die with you: No subject e'er can meet
A nobler fate, than at his sovereign's feet.

   [*Exeunt. Clashing of swords within, and shouts.*]
   [*Enter* **Leonidas, Rhodophil, Palamede, Eubulus, Hermogenes,** *and their* **Party,** *victorious;* **Polydamas** *and* **Argaleon,** *disarmed.*]

Leon. That I survive the dangers of this day,
Next to the gods, brave friends, be yours the honour;
And, let heaven witness for me, that my joy
Is not more great for this my right restored,
Than 'tis, that I have power to recompense
Your loyalty and valour. Let mean princes,
Of abject souls, fear to reward great actions;
I mean to show, that whatsoe'er subjects,
Like you, dare merit, a king, like me, dares give.

Rhod. You make us blush, we have deserved so little.

Pala. And yet instruct us how to merit more.

Leon. And as I would be just in my rewards,
So should I in my punishments; these two,
This, the usurper of my crown, the other,
Of my Palmyra's love, deserve that death,
Which both designed for me.

Poly.   And we expect it.

Arga. I have too long been happy, to live wretched.

Poly. And I too long have governed, to desire
A life without an empire.

Leon. You are Palmyra's father; and as such,
Though not a king, shall have obedience paid
From him who is one. Father, in that name
All injuries forgot, and duty owned.
   [*Embraces him.*]

Poly. O, had I known you could have been this king,
Thus god-like, great and good, I should have wished
To have been dethroned before. 'Tis now I live,

And more than reign; now all my joys flow pure,
Unmixed with cares, and undisturbed by conscience.

        [*Enter* **Palmyra, Amalthea, Artemis, Doralice,** *and* **Melantha**.]

Leon. See, my Palmyra comes! The frighted blood
Scarce yet recalled to her pale cheeks,
Like the first streaks of light broke loose from darkness,
And dawning into blushes. —
        [*To* **Polydamus**.]
        Sir, you said
Your joys were full; Oh, would you make mine so!
I am but half restored without this blessing.

Poly. The gods, and my Palmyra, make you happy,
As you make me!
        [*Gives her hand to* **Leonidas**.]

Palm.   Now all my prayers are heard:
I may be dutiful, and yet may love.
Virtue and patience have at length unravelled
The knots, which fortune tied.

Mela. Let me die, but I'll congratulate his majesty: How admirably well his royalty becomes him! Becomes! That is *lui sied*, but our damned language expresses nothing.

Pala. How? Does it become him already? 'Twas but just now you said, he was such a figure of a man.

Mela. True, my dear, when he was a private man he was a *figure;* but since he is a king, methinks he has assumed another *figure*: He looks so grand, and so august!
        [*Going to* **Leonidas the King**.]

Pala. Stay, stay; I'll present you when it is more convenient. I find I must get her a place at court; and when she is once there, she can be no longer ridiculous; for she is young enough, and pretty enough, and fool enough, and French enough, to bring up a fashion there to be affected.

Leon. [*To* **Rhodophil**.] Did she then lead you to this brave attempt?

[*To* **Amalthea**.]
To you, fair Amalthea, what I am,
And what all these, from me, we jointly owe:
First, therefore, to your great desert we give
Your brother's life; but keep him under guard
Till our new power be settled. What more grace
He may receive, shall from his future carriage
Be given, as he deserves.

Arga. I neither now desire, nor will deserve it;
My loss is such as cannot be repaired,
And, to the wretched, life can be no mercy.

Leon. Then be a prisoner always: Thy ill fate
And pride will have it so: But since in this I cannot,
Instruct me, generous Amalthea, how
A king may serve you.

Amal. I have all I hope,
And all I now must wish; I see you happy.
Those hours I have to live, which heaven in pity
Will make but few, I vow to spend with vestals:
The greatest part in prayers for you; the rest
In mourning my unworthiness.
Press me not farther to explain myself;
'Twill not become me, and may cause your trouble.

Leon. [*Aside*.] Too well I understand her secret grief,
But dare not seem to know it. — Come, my fairest;
　　　　　[*To* **Palmyra**.]
Beyond my crown I have one joy in store,
To give that crown to her whom I adore.

[*Exeunt*.]

EPILOGUE.

Thus have my spouse and I informed the nation,
And led you all the way to reformation;
Not with dull morals, gravely writ, like those,
Which men of easy phlegm with care compose —
Your poets, of stiff words and limber sense,
Born on the confines of indifference;
But by examples drawn, I dare to say,
From most of you who hear and see the play.
There are more Rhodophils in this theatre,
More Palamedes, and some few wives, I fear:
But yet too far our poet would not run;
Though 'twas well offered, there was nothing done.
He would not quite the women's frailty bare,
But stript them to the waist, and left them there:
And the men's faults are less severely shown,
For he considers that himself is one.
Some stabbing wits, to bloody satire bent,
Would treat both sexes with less compliment;
Would lay the scene at home; of husbands tell,
For wenches, taking up their wives i' the Mall;
And a brisk bout, which each of them did want,
Made by mistake of mistress and gallant.
Our modest author thought it was enough
To cut you off a sample of the stuff:
He spared my shame, which you, I'm sure, would not,
For you were all for driving on the plot:
You sighed when I came in to break the sport,
And set your teeth when each design fell short.
To wives and servants all good wishes lend,
But the poor cuckold seldom finds a friend.
Since, therefore, court and town will take no pity,
I humbly cast myself upon the city.

EDITOR'S NOTE

I first stumbled onto *Marriage à-la-Mode* around the year 2005. I don't remember exactly how it happened that I came upon it, but I think it was resulting from an effort to find an obscure and public-domain English comedy to propose for performance at the Santa Fe Playhouse (which never yet has accepted one of my proposals, I may add.) I read the script and loved it, but, as I began arranging it for the theater proposal I discovered a great obstacle to any performances -- the music basically didn't exist. No copies of the sheet music were in print.

While cutting the songs might be easy, since they're really about as relevant to the plot as the tunes in your average Bollywood, the lack of even an option to include them was a bother to me. Luck had it, I'd just had a birthday and relatives had seen to it I possessed a little cash. So, I spent it all in contacting some libraries in Europe, in order to get my hands on the sheet music.

The music was once printed in a book, around the time the play was first performed, called *Choice Songs and Airs for One Voice; to be played on a theorbo-lute or bass viol.* For my efforts to acquire this, I was rewarded -- after some weeks of waiting -- with a stack of images of smudgy, stained old pages with terrible bleed-through. The music, while finally found, was nearly unreadable.

Years passed with me unable to find anyone to help remedy this problem. I admit I can barely read music myself, even if the copy is clean (I've played violin in the past, and know the specific string and finger-position that corresponds to the mark; but I have trouble determining that same note through any other medium.) Efforts to retranscribe the music by myself went nowhere, as I've got no eye for symmetry. The project sat unattended for a long time.

Eventually, I found myself having just a touch of extra money due to the failure of an intended short-film production, which I'd been planning to fund on a budget of a few hundred hoarded-away dollars I had crammed under a lodestone. I decided to use this, instead, to hire someone out to copy the Smith/Staggins music, and figured I could reprint the results so that other people wouldn't wind up like me (and perhaps I could even hope to recoup some tiny percentage of what I did spend.) Unfortunately, when the person who had agreed to do my transcription heard the term "publish" it seems that grand notions of Houghton Mifflin and Random House went to her head, and suddenly she made a hostage of the music, demanding double our agreed upon rate before she would release the work. I was lucky to have paid her nothing upfront and to still have the original copies, and so walked away from the con fairly easy; but still this turn was very disappointing and upsetting to me. I complained to my friends and family, when a stroke of luck came. Adam Davis, a friend of my sister's, came forward offering to transcribe the songs for free. Thank you, Adam! -- it is his transcriptions you find printed here in this book.

As far as I know this is the first time in over 300 years the tunes for "Why Should a Foolish Marriage Vow" and "Whilst Alexis Lay Press'd" have been published. I will be happy if they are put to use.

Talia Felix
July, 2010

TO THE LOVERS OF MUSIC.

Gentlemen and Ladies,

Music is of different effects, and admits of much variety of fancy to please all humors as any science whatsoever. It moves the affections sometimes into a sober composure, and other times into active jollity. These songs and airs are such as were lately composed, and are very suitable and acceptable to the genius of these times. Many of the words have been already published, which gave but little content to diverse ingenious persons, who thought them as dead, unless they had the airy tunes to quicken them; to gratify whom, was a great inducement to me for their publication. The transcriptions of most of these songs were presented to the gentlemen who composed the music, and by them allowed to be made public. And herein likewise, to do the authors right, my care and oversight of the press was not wanting; but notwithstanding all my diligence, some few erratas have passed, both in the words and music, which I desire the ingenious peruser to correct.

Yours,
N.D.

FROM THE ORIGINAL EDITION
CHOICE SONGS AND AYRES FOR ONE VOYCE,
1673.

Why Should a Foolish Marriage Vow

lyrics by John Dryden
music by Robert Smith

transcribed by Adam Davis   layout by Talia Felix

II

*If I have pleasure for a friend
And further joy in store,
What wrong has he whose joys did end,
And who could give no more?
It's a madness that he
Should be jealous of me,
Or that I should bar him of another;
When all we can gain
Is to give ourselves pain,
And neither can hinder the other.*

Whilst Alexis Lay Press'd

lyrics by John Dryden
music by Nicholas Staggins

transcribed by Adam Davis   layout by Talia Felix

II

When Cælia saw this, with a sigh and a kiss,
She cried, "O my Dear! I'm robbed of my bliss!
'Tis unkind to your love and unfaithfully done,
To leave me behind you, and die all alone."

III

The youth, though in haste, and breathing his last,
In pity died slowly, whilst she died more fast;
Till at length she cried "Now my dear, now,
Let's go; Now die my Alexis, and I will die too."

IV

Thus intranced she did lie, while Alexis did try
To recover new breath, that again he might die.
Then often they died, but the more they did so,
The nymph died more quick, and the shepherd more slow.

OTHER BOOKS

'Tis Pity She's a Whore
by John Dryden

Sweeney Todd and the String of Pearls
by James Malcolm Rymer and Thomas Preskett Prest

Fanny Hill
by John Cleland

The Murders in the Rue Morgue
by Edgar Allan Poe

David Garrick: The Play and the Novel
by Thomas William Robertson

La Commedia Inglese: English Commedia dell'Arte Plays
by various authors

Made in the USA
Lexington, KY
16 December 2010